The Come Up

For Men

By Tracy L. Williams

Also By Tracy L. Williams

The Come Up

Urban Development: Adapt or Die

Copyright © 2015 by Tracy L. Williams

All rights reserved. This book or any portion thereof may not be reproduced or used in any manner whatsoever without the express written permission of the publisher except for the use of brief quotations in a book review.

Printed in the United States of America

Cover Design by A'Sista Media Group, LLC

Editor: Ebony Newport

First Printing, 2015

ISBN: 978-0-9881756-7-9

The TLW Group Inc.

INTRODUCTION

We usually define the phrase "being a man" in terms of basic masculinity, rather than something we achieve through lifestyle choices. I took the cues my environment gave me, looked at what the men around me were doing, and blindly followed. I didn't know or care that all these unspoken rules were based on bravado, and the things they encouraged men to do, were often counterproductive. Why would I stop doing all these things that seemed like so much fun? I was having a great time. There was always another party to go to, always more women, and plenty of alcohol to fuel the fires.

Most of all there was that wild feeling of freedom. In some ways it was that immature sense of what freedom is that hurt me most. Real freedom—the kind that gives us strength, and lasts a lifetime-- always comes with responsibility. When we're young most of us underestimate how big a role restraint plays in the successful exercise of freedom. Many of us treat freedom like a credit card with no limits. This goes with the idea that freedom is doing anything we want. But real freedom is more like an investment account. If we simply spend it to run wild, it will soon be gone. But if we keep putting money in, and allow it to grow, we'll have freedom whenever we really need it.

If we see real freedom as the responsibility to choose between right and wrong, then it can lead us to those long-term goals we desire most. This choice between right and wrong is the essence of free will. If we decide to shed all restraint and run amok, free will can be the killer of all our dreams. If we are willing to exercise our freedom in a more constructive way, and we choose to control ourselves, and take positive actions, then we can steer our lives, and the lives of our loved ones, in better directions.

My most disastrous decisions in life resulted from the free will I exercised when I chose to fail. Failure was so easy—a dive that would take me straight down to the bottom. Failure was often accompanied by fun. It came with no apparent responsibilities, no structure, no time-line, and no one to answer to— just a carefree life. Or so it seemed, until reality crashed the party. When you have true freedom, you can choose your path. Without it you have no choice but to take whatever path you come to. Choosing to restrain yourself allows you to have true freedom—freedom that lasts. Making this choice is the most intelligent way to exercise free will.

My life began with a rough childhood littered with bad decisions and horrible results. I wrote about that in my first book, "The Come Up." Now I'm writing the second book in what is becoming a series: "The Come Up for Men." Here I want to go deeper, and explore the process as it applies to men—most specifically young men. Many of the habits I developed in childhood followed me into the world of adults. Some of those habits—and the behaviors they cause—still affect me, but I've learned a lot about controlling myself, and encouraging my positive behaviors. Read on, and you will learn what I learned.

Growing up, I had friends who were only concerned with having a good time. I did what they did. Although I outgrew most of these companions, I still had to live for the rest of my life with the consequences of poor decisions I made in my youth. My promiscuous ways produced many children out of wedlock. Several different mothers had given birth to my children, but wasn't ready to be a father. My irresponsible financial decisions led to maxed-out credit cards, and a mountain of debt. I had to depend on others for the most basic things.

For instance, back when most other people were getting their first cell phones, the cellular companies would only give you a phone if you had good credit. A string of poor decisions, and my immature lifestyle, had eaten away at my credit until there was nothing left. As a result I had to rely on whatever woman I happened to be dating for my cell phone needs. Whatever phone I was using would be in her name, and she was saddled with all the responsibility if I didn't pay. If anything went wrong with the relationship, I had to find another woman with good credit. The same was true with cars, and other credit-based items. Though I was an adult, and supposedly I was free as a bird, I had to rely on the women in my life for many of the things we think of as basics. Because I was often broke, and had no credit, I was dependent on other people, just as a child is dependent on a parent.

Back then I felt as if I had a lot of friends. I thought they were true friends, but that was only because they'd never been put to the test. Whenever trouble arrived, we all ran away and hid until things blew over. None of my "friends" suggested that we face the music, and take responsibility for the damage we'd caused. The idea wouldn't have even occurred to any of us.

In those days I didn't know what true friendship was. I thought of "friends" as being anyone who hung out with me, and ran around with the same people I did. I understood that friendship meant supporting one another, and being loyal, but I didn't really know what that meant. I'd always been taught that loyalty was the glue that held friends together. Later I came to learn that, although this is one aspect of loyalty, it isn't the whole picture. As I began to finally mature, I came to see that the loyalty my friends and I felt towards one another was actually our common commitment to failure.

We were friends for all the wrong reasons. Though I was glad to have these guys at my back, and though I could talk about my troubles to them, when you are on the wrong side of life's equation, none of those things really helps much. We were bound together by failure. Though we'd enrolled in college we seldom showed up for class. This resulted in poor grades, and often failed courses.

We avoided honest work, took pride in our wrongdoing, and chose to live our lives as criminals. We did what real men never do: we turned our backs on our responsibilities, and pretended they weren't even there. In the end we devalued ourselves.

My goal in the following pages is to create a clear-cut definition of what MEN must do to increase their value as people. I want to explore our choices in education, in jobs, in our communities, and in our families. I will look at the kinds of actions we can take to hold ourselves responsible. How can MEN become what they need to be for their families, and communities? Once MEN answer that question, they can join together, and achieve just about anything!

It is my sincere hope that after reading this book, completing the worksheets, and executing the plan, you will become MR. PERFECT!

Chapter One

You Can't Do It Alone!

The Bible is an ancient book written over the course of more than a millennium, with its most recent books (those of the New Testament) arriving on the scene almost two thousand years ago, in the era just after the Crucifixion. The Bible hasn't lost its power, or gone out of date. Most of the quoted passages that follow come from its pages. They help illustrate the principles I'm describing, and my own life experiences. The Bible is still the world's leading source of wisdom, advice, and knowledge. The same basic laws governing life today ruled then as well. The Bible's words still have the same power. Though we've altered the earth around us, explored the planets, and created worldwide systems for instant communication, technology does not change what's human. We still need each other, and when we communicate, we do it with each other. Without other humans, we have nothing.

Psalm 133 tells us: "How good and pleasant it is when brothers live together in unity." Those words were written thousands of years ago, but the idea is just as true today. Today's young men need the support of other good men around them. A reliable trustworthy friend helps keep you positive. Together, good friends can act as checks on each other's more negative tendencies. This enables them to work productively together, getting tasks done better and faster. This truth is expressed in the saying: "Two heads are better than one."

True friendship is the best first step toward achieving your goals. It will help you gather a group of positive, supportive men around you—a group of real friends. You need smart older men who have experience and knowledge, as well as young men like yourself.

A smart man keeps experienced, intelligent, honest advisors close by. He encourages his friends to speak their minds, and suggest worthwhile alternatives.

As you build these kinds of partnerships, make sure you regularly examine your motives. Talk to your friends about why you are on the path that you've chosen. Your goals should be worthwhile, and you must express them clearly to your friends. Talk to these men. Discuss the goals you want to reach. Listen to what your friends have to say about them, and make sure that you are among like-minded men.

Just as we need to make good friends, we also need to be good friends. Once we have found good men who share many of the same goals we do, we must welcome them, and support them. We must listen to their concerns, and give them encouragement whenever things get rough. This doesn't mean that all our friends must always go along with us. Disagreements are inevitable, even among those who are sincerely seeking to live good lives. Sometimes someone will make a mistake, or two people will share the same goal, but disagree on how they might reach it. A wise man understands these things. He knows that two people might see some things differently, and that errors can be forgiven. Forgiveness is the cornerstone of continued growth.

The Bible is full of lessons about disagreements, beginning with the story of Cain and Abel in the Book of Genesis. These sons of Eve both lived off the land. Each brother offered God different sacrifices from his fields. God blessed Abel's offerings, but not Cain's. Cain's jealousy festered, and he grew angry. When Cain allowed his jealous anger to rule him, he killed his brother. This has gone down in human memory as the first murder. God marked Cain, forcing him to carry a curse for the rest of his life.

Another story of extreme jealousy is that of King Saul and David. A part of this story is the passage about David and Goliath.

We have all heard how the young David defeated the Philistine giant, Goliath. David performed this deed with a weapon we usually associate with little boys—a slingshot. David's courage in slaying a giant foe made him a hero.

King Saul saw this, and was jealous of his young subject. Though David was little more than a boy, Saul gave him command of an army of a thousand warriors. King Saul thought this would keep David occupied on the battlefield, and possibly lead to his death, but the young general won battles quickly, and soon returned home, his fame greater than it had ever been. Though a sense of awe at David's accomplishments temporarily overcame Saul's jealously, the King soon began scheming again. King Saul sent David back to fight more Philistines, and when the young man again returned victorious, the King gave him one of his daughters in marriage. Perhaps Saul was thinking like the Don in *The Godfather*, who advised: "Keep your friends close, but keep your enemies closer."

Other wars came, and David once again led armies. When he went on to win countless battles, outshining his envious monarch, Saul began hatching plots to kill his young general. David saw what was coming, and allied himself with King Saul's son, Jonathan. Jonathan was an upright man who disapproved of his father's devious actions.

At some point in our lives nearly all of us find ourselves in similar situations. We must chose between a friend who is wrong and a friend who is right. This is the classic test of loyalty. Does joining with a friend in doing something wrong prove our loyalty? No. A real man is loyal to what is just and right. He surrounds himself with people who share this loyalty to principle.

In the Bible Jonathan went against his father. I come from a background where this simply doesn't happen. Like many other members of my family, I was taught that we were supposed to stand by each other to the death.

An experience I had when I was younger illustrates this attitude: One day, when I was hanging on the corner with a group of my friends, a commotion erupted. One guy showed up, and started trying to rob a second guy. The young man who was the victim of the theft put up a fight. At first he was able to temporarily stop his assailant. But then a few of the thief's friends materialized, seemingly out of nowhere.

We later learned that all of these young men had grown up together. They were from two separate families, but they lived in the same neighborhood. Though what we were seeing appeared to be a simple case of theft, we would soon find out that the theft was one tiny part of a neighborhood family feud.

As members of both families struggled to stop the fighting, I could hear one older man trying to get them to quiet down long enough to figure out what it was all about. When the fighting finally came to a halt, the victim pointed at the robber, saying; "He tried to rob me, but when I fought back, all his cousins came outta nowhere and started in on me."

"I don't understand," said the older man. He turned to the young man's assailants. "This was a fight between your cousin, and this young man. Now, you knew your cousin was robbing him. You knew he was doing wrong. So why are you helping him?"

When they answered, I recognized their response. I'd heard the words more times than I could remember among my own relatives: "I don't care what he did! He's my family and no one is going to do anything to him while I'm around... period!"

"Family" should be a serious bond formed from blood ties, and/or long, deep personal connections. Family members should be loyal to one another. They should support each other in all their constructive enterprises. But this loyalty shouldn't be blind or unconditional. Genuine loyalty must be coupled with justice. If I'm doing wrong, and you help me do it, that's not real loyalty; it's unthinking, ignorant allegiance.

A truly loyal friend would ask you to stop and think, and consider issues of right-and-wrong in the situation.

In Mathew 12:46-50, Jesus chose those who were willing to follow the word of His Father over His mother and brothers. In this passage Matthew writes: "While Jesus was still talking to the crowd, his mother and brothers stood outside, wanting to speak to him. Someone told him, 'Your mother and brothers are standing outside, wanting to speak to you.' He replied to him, 'Who is my mother, and who are my brothers?' Pointing to his disciples, he said, 'Here are my mother and my brothers. For whoever does the will of my Father in heaven is my brother and sister and mother.'"

In these examples we see strong decent men who have dedicated their lives to doing the right thing. When David became King of Israel, he appointed Jonathan as his second-in-command, paying the debt he owed to this man for putting loyalty to principle above his feelings about his own father. We don't need to explain the action of Jesus, our Savior, as he talks to his followers. Christ's life speaks for itself throughout the New Testament. You must ask yourself: Who among the men you hang with will choose what is right and just? And will these friends hold you accountable for your own actions? Together will you and your friends keep each other righteous and honest? Those are the questions you should ask when deciding whether a person is your friend.

The second Book of Samuel tells us about three "mighty men" whom David came to depend on. All three of these men defended their King and country, risking their lives so the Kingdom of Israel could survive and flourish. These men understood what was right, and they defended their country so that the principles they lived by would endure. Who among your friends would qualify to be called "mighty men?"

Though some immature minds think masculinity is all about brute strength and power, in truth the qualities of compassion and forgiveness are just as essential to real manhood. The Bible has plenty to say about this. Another Genesis passage tells the story of Jacob's youngest son, Joseph. Like many youngest children, Joseph was favored by his father, Jacob. This made Joseph's older brothers jealous. They plotted against him, trying to cause his downfall. Finally they had the opportunity to sell him as a slave to Egyptian traders. Joseph's "owners" resold him in Egypt, where he wound up as a servant in the house of the Pharaoh.

In the house of that most powerful ruler Joseph revealed his ability to interpret dreams. When the Pharaoh's butler and baker were imprisoned, both told Joseph their dreams. Joseph told them the dreams were signs pointing to the butler's release and the hanging of the baker. When his predictions proved accurate, the news reached the ear of the Pharaoh. The Pharaoh called Joseph to his side, and gave him a dream to interpret. Joseph's advice was so good and sensible that the Pharaoh made the young man his chief adviser.

Joseph could not only interpret dreams; he had an unerring instinct for knowing what to do when they came true. His gift of foresight helped him plan and manage huge enterprises. As the Pharaoh came to rely on this young man's judgment, he also gave Joseph more and more responsibility for managing the country's land and resources. When Joseph's predictions and planning helped Egypt avoid the effects of a region-wide famine, the Pharaoh appointed him chief administrator of the entire realm. These were seven good years that Joseph had said were coming. As he had predicted, Egypt's farmers had record grain harvests, each bigger than the last. Joseph saw to it that they saved a percentage of their grain to insure against poor yields in years when their fields would lie parched and fallow. When the lean years came, and people in the lands bordering Egypt were threatened with starvation, Egypt's ample stockpiles of grain allowed its population to survive and thrive. They even had enough to feed people from neighboring countries.

That's why Joseph's brothers eventually came to Egypt. They hoped to find food for their people back in Israel. When they realized that the man in charge was their banished brother, they feared he would seek revenge for what they had done to him. He did not. He welcomed them, forgave them for their transgressions, and then gave them plenty of supplies for their families and households.

Joseph is a fine example of a man of outstanding character. Few would have blamed him if he'd held a grudge, and punished his brothers. But he didn't. Most of us would understand, and even admire him simply for forgiving them for their crime against him. We would be impressed even if he'd just given them enough food for the long road home.

Joseph went far beyond that, treating his brothers as loyal, decent men who must be respected, and given a real chance. He even provided them with jobs. These jobs weren't mere gifts; they were tasks that came with substantial powers and responsibilities. Most of us would say that Joseph had very good reasons to reject his brothers, and harshly punish them. Though he'd risen to an exalted status, he might have recalled that his brothers had considered killing him out of sheer jealousy. They had thrown him into a pit and let him starve while they decided his fate. Instead of killing him, they'd chosen to sell him for profit, assuming he would spend the rest of his life in abject slavery, far away from their homes.

Joseph had lived as a slave before his new masters noticed his abilities. He knew life at the bottom, as well as life at the top. Joseph had done very well, but if his brothers had known that he was going to be such a success, they probably would've decided to kill him.

Some of us hold grudges about the most menial things. We lose years of valuable friendship over matters that should be easily reconciled. We cut ourselves off from each other, magnifying each other's faults and sins. If you find yourself doing this, take a timeout. Let your anger cool, and imagine the things that you both could accomplish if you could just get that grudge out of the way. If you can forgive others, and make enemies into friends, they will help you reach your goals.

The stories from Scripture show us how men can pull together into productive groups, and achieve wealth and power to use for the good of their communities. This brings me back to a theme I explored in my first book, "The Come Up." There I cited the author, Napoleon Hill, and his concept of the mastermind. Hill's contention was this: When liked-minded men come together with the purpose of achieving a goal, and they are in perfect harmony, nothing can stop them. This can only be achieved if all members are men of virtue, and are committed to what is just and right. If one member has devious goals and ulterior motives it weakens the collective group. The adage, "A chain fence is only as strong as its weakest link," is true, and applies to this situation.

The conclusion we should draw from all this is that a man should be loyal to what is just and right. His loyalty to his family will be strongest if it is also just and right. A man should be compassionate and forgiving. He must be dedicated to his mastermind, and commit himself to achieving his goals.

Questions:

1. What are some challenges and or difficulties that you have overcome or are in the process of overcoming? What have you done (or will do) to overcome these challenges?

_____
_____
_____
_____
_____
_____
_____
_____
_____
_____
_____
_____
_____
_____
_____
_____
_____

2. What are your goals?

_____
_____
_____
_____
_____
_____
_____
_____
_____
_____
_____
_____
_____

3. What are your friends' goals?

_____
_____
_____
_____
_____
_____
_____

4. Do they align to give you the greatest chance for success?

_____
_____

In the following pages you will find questions at the end of every chapter. Your responses to them will help you gauge yourself and your mastermind. Answer the questions honestly and truthfully. Your answers will become the foundation of any statement you make about your values, and your mission in life. Here we have looked at the initial changes you must make if you are going to truly commit yourself to building a more productive and prosperous life. Understanding those changes is what separates leaders from followers and men from boys.

When I was in my teens I had my first inkling that my friends weren't giving me much of anything. To be fair, I wasn't giving them much either. Each day we hung out, drinking, driving, and sometimes beating up people who offended our warped sensibilities. Though we didn't have much in the way of values, we did have a sense that we should stick together, so we formed a gang.

As gang members we often drove around our neighborhoods, always with several of us in the car. None of us had a license, but we didn't let that stop us. We would steal cars, "borrow" cars, or find someone old enough to drive. Once we were out there on the street we would cruise until we saw a likely victim—usually a kid from a rival gang. We would then jump out of the car, catch him, and start beating him up. One time a cop caught us in the act. We ran, and two of us got away, but I was one of the four they put in jail.

When the police called our parents, we knew we were in big trouble. Yet we didn't really feel the threat. Right there in the holding pen we began to celebrate. What were we celebrating? We had just been arrested, and now we all had permanent records. They set $100 bail on each of us. As the hours passed, and the celebration cooled, one-by-one my friends' parents came and got them. Finally the only one left was me. My only companions were my thoughts. As the alcohol drained out of my system, I wondered how I had gotten myself into this situation. My gang was no help to me now. They weren't going to raise my bail, or get me a lawyer.

This gang subtracted from my progress, and added to my demise. The comfort I got from fitting in with them blinded me to my real needs.

Years passed, but the lesson faded. Even in my young adulthood I continued to act in ways that were bound to haunt my life far into my future. Some of the causes were in those childhood bonds—I'd never bothered to break them. I felt as if I was getting a better grasp of what life was all about. I thought I was finally getting productive, and I wanted to bring my friends into my efforts. They weren't ready.

With the help of my "friends", I started businesses. Each one failed. I became a partner in a downtown Rochester nightclub. I wanted the popularity that went with owning a glitzy club more than I wanted success. I drank, caroused, and didn't keep my eye on the business. I enjoyed all the perks, and paid no attention to the fundamentals. My partners followed my lead. For a while we had a blast. Enough money came in to allow us to think much more was on the way. We paid almost no attention to bookkeeping or bottom lines. None of us were focused on what really mattered.

My actions were the exact opposite of what was necessary for my long-term well-being. I was a part of a group that was unwittingly dedicating itself to failure. If I'd put the same energy into strategies for success the outcome would have been different, and I would have avoided a lot of misery.

In the New Testament St. Paul wrote: "When I was a child, I talked like a child, I thought like a child, I reasoned like a child. When I became a man, I put the ways of childhood behind me." (1 Corinthians, 13:11) If you are like me, it's taken you some time to put the ways of childhood behind you. Sometimes "ways of childhood" are tied together with friends of childhood. It's one thing to be 6 years old, and to want nothing more than to have a good time. At that age, a good time might be an extra scoop of ice cream. At 16 it's a lot more complicated. By that time you've begun making important choices about right and wrong. If you're not learning the deeper meaning of those choices by the age of 16, you're already in trouble.

At 26 you should understand those choices, and you should be choosing the responsible path for yourself and your loved ones. By this time it should be a habit. Your loyalties and responsibilities should be tied together in everything you do.

If we are going to succeed we must understand what real loyalty is, and choose friends who share that understanding of loyalty. Not only must we share positive values, we must also live those values. Building a group of men who share positive values will give you the best chance to succeed in life. If you answer the following questions, it could be your first step toward finding your core group of men with real, positive values.

QUESTIONS:

5. Who are my top five friends?

_____
_____
_____
_____

6. What does each of them do for a living?

_____
_____
_____
_____
_____
_____

7. How long has each of them been at his current job?

_____
_____
_____
_____
_____
_____

8. Do they have families?   Yes ___ No___

9. How do the fathers among them perform as fathers? (Rate them A to F)

_____
_____
_____
_____
_____
_____
_____
_____

10. How do they treat their spouses? (Rate them A to F)

_____
_____
_____
_____
_____
_____
_____
_____

11. Do they share similar ethical, moral and value systems?
    Yes___ No___

12. Can they hold you accountable to achieve your goals?
    Yes___ No___

Chapter Two

What Is Your Goal In Life?

It's easy to set goals, but much harder to reach them. You can wake up in the morning and set a dozen goals before breakfast. All of these might be good, righteous, honorable goals whose accomplishment would bring benefits to you and those around you. These goals also might be realistic, logical and attainable. But then you have to reach them. If they are small and simple things like: "We're going to have scrambled eggs for breakfast this morning," then you don't have a problem. Reaching such a goal takes only about as much time and effort as setting it. But if your dozen goals include success in business, marrying the right woman, and creating a solid, loving family, then it's going to take a little longer. We might set goals like these this morning, but taking them to heart, and sincerely trying to reach them requires soul-searching, and a lifetime of commitment. To achieve goals like these you must use firm determination to build a solid foundation, and then execute a never-ending follow-through.

That's a lot to ask this early in the book, so let's go back to breakfast for a moment. After all, though it doesn't take much effort to scramble those eggs, it's a necessary task with a well-defined goal. Reaching any goal, large or small, requires energy and good health. In their book, "The Power of Full Engagement," authors Jim Loehr and Tony Schwartz argue that we should see all human endeavors, including business, in terms of the energy we put into them. The key is to manage that energy so that we use it well, and waste as little as possible. They feel energy should supplant time as our main concern in everything we do. Time goes forward consistently no matter what, but energy is a finite resource that we can manage and change.

One activity Loehr and Schwartz promote is a healthy diet made up of 5 or 6 smaller meals rather than 2 or 3 big ones. The first of these should be a healthy breakfast. It's an excellent first goal every single day. You should have foods high in protein (dairy products, soy products or meat), vitamins (fruits and juices), and, as long as they don't add pounds, carbohydrates (cereals). (You'll read a detailed discussion of diet and workout in Chapter 6.) Once you've eaten a well-balanced breakfast, you will have the energy to put your mastermind to work on larger, longer-term goals.

When you set goals, you should also make a definite, sensible plan to accomplish them. Any such plan should have a starting date. If these goals are worthwhile, that date should be today. If you can't physically begin the tasks, you can study the situation, and plan.

Today is the day when you are setting the goal in your mind, so there should be something you can do today to solidify your commitment, and start moving toward your destination. It may be as simple as writing out your plan, but reaching goals requires more than planning. If you can begin putting your thoughts into actions, no matter how small, you will have taken that essential first step toward reaching your aims. A good first step makes every further step a little easier. Without it, your plan is still nothing more than a plan.

If a goal is going to be attainable it must be something you can embrace wholeheartedly. While the goal might seem improbable to some, it must be possible and desirable—you have to want it. For instance, if you're less than six feet tall, and don't much like basketball, there's no point in trying to become an NBA all-star. However, if you're a fast, football-loving five-eleven, who's already been a top running back in high school, moving on to star in college and the NFL are possibilities. People around you will say that your goal is improbable, and they'll be right. But you can shift the odds in your favor by getting up every day, and dedicating your whole heart, body, mind and soul to becoming the best player you can be. So the first rule in settling your goals is to aim for goals that you truly want to reach. The second rule is that a goal must be physically possible.

The world of sports provides clear-cut examples of goals, and how to reach them. A young man looks at a game he knows well, sees an athlete he admires playing a position the young man has played himself. The young man then sets the goal of playing that position in the big leagues. The best athletes always have a set of goals: making the team, becoming a starter, hitting .300 and winning the pennant, rushing 2,000 yards and winning that Super Bowl ring, or scoring 30 points a game and getting into the playoffs. A minor leaguer aims at breaking into the majors. A superstar won't feel complete until he's been voted MVP. A heavyweight won't stop boxing until he's won the championship. Each goal is focused, and easily identifiable. However, in most of life's everyday activities, measurements of progress are a little hazier.

What if you are a jobless young man with no money, a troubled past, and only a tenth-grade education? If this is you, setting goals should be easy. When you're starting from the bottom, your only alternatives are to stay where you are, or do something to make your life better. On any given day your immediate goal might be as simple as getting a job—any job. While this is a reasonable goal for a young man with nothing, it's also short-term. What happens when you get the job? Are there further goals? Does the job have a future? Are you learning any skills? Or is this a minimum wage job guaranteed to lead you nowhere?

"Let the thief no longer steal, but rather let him labor, doing honest work with his own hands, so that he may have something to share with anyone in need."

Ephesians 4:28

Many unemployed young men see a job only as a temporary source of legitimate income. Like myself, and the guys I once hung with, a lot of these men prefer to make money in other, less honest, but more profitable ways. They might deal drugs, run scams, or rob people and businesses. To a man who does these things, a legitimate job is just a way of guaranteeing a steady paycheck. Sometimes the job is more like a cover story than a real occupation. No one is ever surprised when a man with a job has money. We assume he earned his cash. But when a man hasn't worked in a year, and his unemployment ran out months ago, a wad of cash draws attention—usually unwanted attention. Men in this position often have only minor, short-term goals, like avoiding getting caught for one more day.

Worthwhile goals almost always require some sacrifice. You have to work hard, and often you must give up some of your youthful pleasures. In their book authors Loehr and Schwartz outline a program that some would see as giving up almost everything. They subscribe to Benjamin Franklin's idea of "early to bed, early to rise." They recommend a break from work every ninety minutes, but this break should involve physical activity. They feel a successful regimen should include at least two full workouts every week. While these worthwhile goals may seem to take up your time and limit your fun, they also increase your energy, give you stamina, and sharpen your focus. These are sacrifices with payoffs, and one of the first payoffs might be success in finding a job.

A job is a worthwhile goal, but some jobs are more worthwhile than others. One goal a man should aim for is to work at something that has real value. This could be a job in sales, or a job-training program for a trade or profession. It might be a service job, or a government, or church-sponsored position. "Worthwhile" doesn't necessarily mean social work, or religious occupations. Much of a job's value can be purely financial. Making money honestly is financially beneficial. If you use that money to pay for your family's needs, the job's financial benefits become something more. These benefits can help you create a safe, secure environment for your children. They can pay for education, a better house, and better health care.

We can all name jobs that appear to be good and worthwhile. Teachers, clergy, healthcare workers, and emergency responders fit into this category. Jobs like these don't make people rich, though they do provide reasonably good paychecks. If you're going to do well in positions like these, your goals must include intangibles like wisdom, happiness, and hope.

This is where personality enters into the mix. A man might become a teacher because one of his teachers was his hero. Maybe his 10th grade biology teacher made science come alive for him. This inspiration compels the young man to set a goal: To be like that biology teacher. The road might not be straight or easy. The young man might be led astray, as I was. After getting himself back on track, he might fall deeply into debt while getting a good education. He might have failed relationships with women, and problems with his family. But if his dedication to his goal is sincere, and if he has the ability, he can struggle past these obstacles, and eventually stand in front of a class, inspiring them, just as his biology teacher inspired him. He might not be teaching biology. His subject might be history, or math, or science. But if he believes in what he's doing, and if he does it well, this young man reaches his most important goal every day: he helps his students create a better future.

A passage from the Old Testament tells us:

"Even youths grow tired and weary, and young men stumble and fall; but those who hope in the Lord will renew their strength.
They will soar on wings like eagles; they will run and not grow weary, they will walk and not be faint."
                                                        Isaiah 40:30-31

Though our aspiring teacher's goal wouldn't be there without the inspiration his teacher gave him, he should still have financial aspirations. Though teachers don't make huge salaries, many make enough to save regularly once their student loans are paid. Most teaching jobs offer benefits, including health, and often a reasonable pension program. Some teachers find lucrative sidelines to fill the summer months. Though few teachers get rich, some do, and the rest can live comfortably while knowing that they are helping others have happy lives.

Another man might train to be an emergency responder because of a similar inspiration: a responder who was his hero. Maybe he saw one of these heroes save a loved one. A man like this one likes to help people, but his talents are for dealing with crisis situations. When fire breaks out, or cars crash, or something blows up, this is the guy we want to see. His success is easy to gauge. We can measure it in saved lives, healed wounds, and homes that are still standing.

Financially the emergency responder is probably a lot like the teacher. He can live a reasonably good life, but he's not likely to become the richest man in town. When he's just starting out, his financial goals should begin with his paycheck, and with his expectations he has for his career path. In most cases, this is not hard to figure out. If he's been hired by his local fire department, and has trained to be a firefighter, he can learn the pay scales of all the departmental jobs simply by looking it up in public records. There will be the base pay for each position, perks and benefits, such as vacation, sick leave, and pension, and there will be the possibility of overtime hours. Our firefighter might examine the benefits of seniority and promotion. He might be happy with his firefighting job, and simply want to stay a long time, building up seniority, or maybe he wants to be his city's fire chief one day. Whatever his goals are, they should align with his future wants and needs, and with the needs of his family.

Public service jobs like these have the most appeal for men who are more concerned with security than amassing a huge fortune. The rewards of these jobs can be huge in terms of human value—people helped, lives improved, and problems solved. The financial rewards are enough to live the middle class American Dream. A teacher or firefighter who is careful with his money can buy a house, educate his children, and even have a little left for investing in the future. If he invests wisely, he should be able to retire early, and find new challenges. When he reaches that age, he'll be able to look back and see that he reached his goal because he set his sights on it many years earlier. That decision gave him the focus and vision to achieve what he set out to achieve.

Work in the private sector can be just as fulfilling for a man who prefers the free-range activities that go with entrepreneurship. Many young men who leave school early wind up working construction. For some it's just one more job in a long string of them, but other men love the work of building things. Most of the ones who stick around long enough to learn a skill get some enjoyment from what they're doing. It's natural to feel pride in a job well done, and in construction we can see the jobs we've done at the end of every day.

Many a man has been inspired to become a carpenter, electrician, or

roofer after working as a helper on a construction site from start to finish. That's when he can look at the completed structure, and say: "I helped build that."

That electrician might be perfectly happy to be an electrician. A skilled electrician can make $70,000 per year, with even more for overtime hours. Even without benefits, that's a paycheck most of us would see as worthwhile. The carpenter can do just as well, but what if he has the kind of personality that wants to achieve more? What if he's filled with the entrepreneurial spirit? The carpenter might be willing to risk his savings to start his own construction company. This is when setting one's goals takes on extra dimensions.

"I know how to be brought low, and I know how to abound;
in any and all circumstances, I have learned the secret of facing plenty and hunger, abundance and need. I can do all things in him who strengthens me."

Philippians 4:12-13

St. Paul wrote to the Philippians about how we all need God's help to do anything worthwhile. He noted that God works through all of us, so when we look for God's help, we will often find that he acts through the people around us. Paul told also his readers: "Let each of you look not only to your own interests, but also to the interests of others." (Corinthians 2:4) New businesses always involve the interests of others. You are the one providing a product or service, but if you're going to succeed, you must convince others to pay for it. In most businesses, you will also need others (your employees, suppliers, and service providers) to help you operate.

When a man starts a business with the intent of seeing that business succeed and grow, he is taking on a new and different responsibility. The firefighter is responsible for life-and-death decisions every day. The teacher is responsible to his students and their parents, and must do all he can to help them create a better future. The entrepreneur starts out with a responsibility to himself and his dream of success, but once he has taken steps to begin his business, his responsibilities widen.

Even before the carpenter strikes out on his own, he must learn these responsibilities. One of the best ways to do this is to observe the people who employ him now. What are his boss's responsibilities? Does his boss fulfill his obligations, or does he cut corners? Does this boss treat employees fairly? Does he manage the job well? Does this result in high-quality buildings? Over years in construction, most employees work for many different employers. A carpenter in this position might have observed several bosses closely. He should learn from what they do right, but he should also watch for lessons when they do something wrong. One might have skimped on lumber. Another might have paid off corrupt inspectors to overlook shoddy work. A third might be an excellent employer, looking out for the people he's hired, reassuring his clients, and putting up well-constructed buildings that will stand the test of time. If the carpenter takes this third boss as his role model, he is setting the goal of becoming a boss who's just as good, and he is committing himself to the responsibilities inherent in that goal.

Soon the carpenter is studying websites, and talking to former co-workers who've struck out on their own. He's estimating what he will need to start. He and his young wife have saved $15,000, but he soon realizes he will need much more. He's going to start out as a carpentry subcontractor, hiring one other, somewhat less experienced carpenter, and two helpers. He needs a van, tools, and other basics. To keep his three employees paid and happy, he also needs operating capital. When he cuts every extra expense, but assumes the first six months will be rocky, he comes up with a figure of $45,000. He thinks this much cash will give him enough time, and buy him enough necessities, to get his fledgling business off the ground.

The carpenter's initial goal is to find financial resources. When he talks to his bank, he learns that they will only lend him another $15,000 to match his own funds. He thinks their interest rate is a little high, so he begins to look elsewhere. He goes to a businessman in his neighborhood, but this man is only interested in investing if he can own a majority share, and control the company. "Of course, I don't know construction, so I would leave all the day-to-day operations to you," he assures the carpenter.

The carpenter doesn't believe this. He's seen that most business investors eventually find reasons to take control of their investments.

Finally he hears that an old high school friend now makes his living as a venture capitalist—someone who provides start-up funds for new businesses, normally for a share of future profits. The carpenter goes to this old classmate, not really expecting much. But this potential investor recognizes and appreciates the possibilities in the carpenter's business plan. He's willing to invest $10,000, and help the carpenter get a larger bank loan at lower interest. The carpenter will still own 51%, and his high school friend will own the minority share of 49%. This friend is willing to trust the carpenter. This kind of trust is essential in any successful business.

Once the plan is in motion, the carpenter is free to operate his business. However, along with that privilege come many responsibilities He's responsible to his wife, his friend, his bank, and his employees. He sets up an office in his home, creates a website, and lists a phone number and email address for his business. He announces his new business through mailings and calls to every general contractor in the area. He also targets homeowners in particular neighborhoods.

Once he's told the public about his new business, our carpenter accepts his last, and greatest responsibility: his obligation to the community. He begins fulfilling this obligation by conducting his business legally, honestly, and ethically. A good businessman recognizes that, as long as his community provides him with a chance to succeed, he owes an intangible debt. He must pay it by giving back to the community. This is the responsibility of everyone who conducts business with others.

An entrepreneur who avoids these obligations might make money. He might cut corners, underpay his workers, bribe inspectors, and falsify documents. It's possible that he will see financial profits from every wrongful act he commits. He might wind up with a huge fortune from always doing the wrong thing. That does happen occasionally. However most of the entrepreneurs who make a habit of doing bad things fail miserably in the end.

They might ride high for a while, but soon enough most of them lose their fortunes to poor management, back taxes, fines, and legal expenses.

Many irresponsible entrepreneurs wind up in jail, while others are reduced to poverty. Their businesses fail, their marriages falter, and in the end they are forgotten, or become objects of pity. Why? These entrepreneurs were only in it for the money, and for the prestige and power that go with owning a business. When we fail to understand our responsibilities, we pay for it with dashed hopes and shattered dreams.

Our carpenter avoids becoming one of these failures. At each point in his start-up process, he's understood his long-term goal, and all the responsibilities that go with it. As he's invested all the money he and his wife have saved, and accepted his friend's venture capital, and taken a loan from the bank, he's committed himself to making these investments turn a profit. When he posts his first online ad, he knows that he will owe each and every client the best work possible. These debts are on his mind when he hires his second carpenter and the two helpers. His first year will be difficult, and his second year won't be a lot easier, but he does good work, learns from his mistakes, and in the long run our carpenter will surpass his original financial goals, and achieve much more. He will earn the appreciation and respect of all around him.

QUESTIONS:

Check one answer for each question:

1. When setting a long-term goal, which of these issues should be the most important?

a. Fringe benefits ___

b. Quick profits ___

c. Friends' opinions ___

d. Responsibilities to others ___

2. When you accept investment capital from others, you should:

a Spend it quickly on whatever you like ___

b. Spend it carefully on items in your business plan ___

c. Keep it all in the bank until it's time to repay your investors ___

d. Look for a way to double it quickly so you can pay off your investors, and keep the rest for yourself and your family ___

3. If you don't want to be an entrepreneur:

a. You should accept the fact that you will probably be unemployed most of the time ___

b. You should train for, and find a job you like, preferably one that inspires you ___

c. You should take the first job you find, and make an effort to like it ___

d. You should stop worrying, and do whatever your friends are doing ___

Chapter 3

Getting started: Personal Inventory

"Every athlete exercises self-control in all things. They do it to receive a perishable wreath, but we an imperishable. So I do not run aimlessly; I do not box as one beating the air. But I discipline my body and keep it under control, lest after preaching to others I myself should be disqualified."

1 Corinthians 9:25-27

The marathon is unique among sports events. Like most foot races, it seems simple at first. There's a starting line, a set route, and a finish line. Multiple contestants take off from the starting line in heats. They run the set route, and many of them finish. The one who reaches the finish line first is declared the winner.

But the marathon defies simplicity, beginning with one basic fact: its length. Runners must cover just over 26.2 miles. Even the fastest contestants need more than two hours to reach the finish, and a lot can happen. The routes of modern marathons usually weave through central cities, with twists, turns, loops, and the occasional traffic circle. In the most popular marathons, like Boston and New York, the enthusiastic crowds sometimes confuse things further, spilling onto streets, where—whether intentionally or inadvertently—they interfere with the race's progress.

This complexity has been known to inspire cheating. In 1980 Rosie Ruiz crossed the Boston Marathon's finish line in record time. The judges then declared her the winner of the women's division. When observers noted that her legs seemed flabbier than a well-trained runner's ought to be, and she wasn't winded or sweaty, some questioned her right to keep her trophy. In interviews, she couldn't recall seeing landmarks along the route; a vast and unusual neighborhood had totally escaped her notice: she couldn't remember a particularly crowded stretch. Suddenly witnesses came forward saying they'd seen her on the subway at times when she said she had been running. In the end Ms. Ruiz was disqualified. She had taken advantage of a race so long, and so crowded, that no one could even keep track of the leaders. She had made fools of the organizers, but she suffered for it. When her fraud was confirmed she was forever banned from competing in the Boston and New York races.

That huge crowd of contestants is the other unique thing about a marathon. Though these courses are more than twice as long as those for any other standard foot race, American marathons attract larger numbers of contestants than more reasonable runs of 10 miles, or even 10 kilometers (about 6.2 miles). Over two million Americans try to run a marathon each year, and over a half a million cross the finish line. The (approximately) 13.1-mile half-marathon has recently surpassed the marathon in finishers, but many of these shorter contests are the first sections of marathons where runners are given the chance to opt out, and still get an official finishing time for a race, albeit a much shorter one. So some dedicated marathon enthusiasts see these half-length contests as mere excuses for people who don't have enough endurance to last to the end.

No footrace draws more spectators than the marathon. Most of these fans come to see friends and relatives who are running the race. Marathon runners who have competed in other sports claim that fan support along the way is more important in a marathon than in any other physical competition. So, though this might seem like a sport celebrating individual effort, the most successful marathoners know that their victories can never happen without teamwork. (One detail about Ms. Ruiz was that during the race many people had spotted her somewhere other than the route, but the only witnesses to her running were at the start and the finish line. She didn't have a team.)

The marathon runner puts together this team while he's training. If he's serious, and proves that he's worth supporting, often a team will form around him. This might make it sound as if building a team is effortless, but nothing could be further from the truth. This young man is working 24/7 to reach a high-profile goal. Each day he runs mile after mile. He eats a strict diet, keeps a tight schedule, and tends to every physical problem and need. If he's a truly competitive athlete he runs other races. He might have an interested coach helping him, and he often has lots of family and friends supporting him. Most marathons are purely amateur, with no scholastic or professional backers, so all of this support must come from private efforts. The enterprise of running a marathon doesn't automatically involve a school gym, or a club's equipment rooms, locker rooms, or support staff. It's usually an independent venture. The young man has his two feet, and the team of fans who support him. These people help him train because they believe in him.

When a young man decides to turn his life around, he must approach this goal like the runner approaching the marathon. He must train. He must look into his personal inventory, and find the tools and resources he needs to get to his goal. He must schedule his tasks and exercises, plan his program for success, and follow through on it every day. When he needs help, he shouldn't be too proud or embarrassed to ask for it. When this happens, he should look at the people around him, and choose those who are positive, able, and true. If he does this, he will soon have a team of supporters who stand by him through thick and thin. He will attract this team by proving his willingness to change his life. He will keep their support and loyalty by proving that he fully intends to stay on this path.

As the young man looks into the future, what does he have that will attract a team like this? What's in his personal inventory? If you are in this position, you must look into your future, identify your goals (as we went over in the last chapter), and honestly examine what qualities, skills, and training you will use to reach them. These are the attributes you bring to your efforts. These qualities will see you through difficult challenges, and inspire others to help you. Though you may have to search for them, you must also have faith that these attributes exist. They are there in your personal inventory.

First and foremost are your personal qualities. These are the basic building blocks of who you are—the core of your identity. Don't make the mistake of confusing your core personal qualities with your past behavior. If you are reading this book to learn how to change your future, there's a strong possibility that you've done things in the past that you now regret. Almost everyone has regrets. If your regret is real, and you sincerely want to turn your life around, that desire is your first building block in your efforts to create a better future—the foundation for all the rest. It is the personal quality that allows other qualities to come through. You've made mistakes, paid a price, and rather than giving into to anger and bitterness, you are learning from what you've done. You should understand that you haven't learned everything. It takes a lifetime to learn all the lessons our mistakes can teach us, but the time to start is now. As long as you understand that, you can begin learning from past behavior and applying those lessons to all of your efforts to build a brighter, happier life.

"Finally, brothers, whatever is true, whatever is honorable, whatever is just, whatever is pure, whatever is lovely, whatever is commendable, if there is any excellence, if there is anything worthy of praise, think about these things.
What you have learned and received and heard and seen in me—practice these things, and the God of peace will be with you."

Philippians 4: 8-9

What else do you have besides a desire to do things right this time? Are you honest? Thrifty? Generous? Alert? Patient? Though some of these qualities can't be taught, if you have the seeds of them within you, they can be developed, sharpened, and finally, taken to heart.

Of the things I've mentioned above, the most difficult to deal with is honesty. Honesty is the key to any personal inventory. Honesty is there in all of us, but sometimes we lose track of it. When we do we must rebuild the habits of honesty. The best way to start doing this is to make sure you're being honest with yourself. That's not as simple, or as easy, as it sounds.

When looking at your own ideas, beliefs, and opinions, honesty requires objectivity. Objectivity is the ability to step back from something, and see the whole of it without prejudice of any kind. Perfect objectivity is impossible, but a basic, sensible objectivity is something anyone can develop.

It begins with clearing your mind. You must try to erase all feelings, judgments, and attitudes. To be truly objective you want to step back from your thoughts, and look at them as if they were entirely new to you. You can see an example of how this works in Chapter One. There we looked at the nature of loyalty. When we're young and immature, we tend to think of loyalty as something that's absolute. A child thinks of loyalty to his family as a rigid, unbending principle that requires total support for all family members, and from them as well, at all times. An immature teenager might think of his gang the same way.

But what happens if one of your brothers steals cash from another brother? Who deserves your support? You might see this one as easy: the thief has put himself outside the family, so your loyalty goes to the victim. But then the thief says the victim wasn't a victim at all. What if he claims this brother owed him money, and had promised to pay him back with this cash. What if the thief has an IOU signed by the so-called victim? And what if the so-called victim claims he already paid the cash, and that the thief promised to return the IOU, but never did?

Blind loyalty won't help you here. As we saw in Chapter One, real, true loyalty is too complicated to be blind. Real loyalty demands that you find the truth, and act in a righteous way. If you add compassion to this principle, you will encourage truth and righteousness in your brothers and friends. In our example your obligation to both of your brothers requires you to exercise the ultimate loyalty: that which we give to the truth.

Difficult as it might seem, at times like this you must put aside your feelings, and look at the evidence objectively. Which brother's story sounds more sensible? Are there any witnesses to the disputed transactions? Does the IOU look real? Is it dated? Are there any other documents that support the either side? Once you see the truth, you have a duty to support the righteous brother, and to correct the brother who's done wrong.

This is a classic case of how objectivity works. Objectivity's only aim is truth. To get to the truth, you must distance yourself from your brothers, and allow the evidence to speak for itself.

That means *all* of the evidence. Though you need to step away from your feelings for these brothers, you can't ignore their past behavior. If one brother has constantly been truthful with you throughout your life, and the other has been known to lie, objectivity dictates that you consider that history. The more objective you are, the better your chances of learning what really happened. It's a case where you're judging the honesty of others, but the quality of your judgment depends entirely on your honesty with yourself.

Honesty is the most basic quality inside of any human being. No one can teach you to be an honest person, but if you have honesty in you (as virtually everyone does), you can train yourself in habits of objectivity. Whenever someone tells you something important, if you have any questions at all, ask. Don't be afraid of appearing ignorant. We are all ignorant of many things, which is why we must ask questions. Remember: the only stupid question is the one you didn't ask. Examine the answers to see if they fit with the things you already know. Does this information line up with the information you received before? Has this person given you truthful answers in the past? Does this person have opinions or feelings that distort his point of view? How much objectivity does he have?

If someone tells you something false, you should figure out whether he has intentionally lied to you, or if he's simply made a mistake. Objectivity is your most essential tool in doing this. If he's making false statement on purpose, he's being dishonest. If it's simply a mistake, then you may still trust this person's intentions, even if you don't always trust his judgment.

These are some of the exercises we do every day to encourage the habits of honesty. The habits can be learned, but the honesty must come from inside us. Qualities like thrift, generosity, patience, and focus are easier to develop through habitual practice. Having an inner sense about them helps a lot, but you can improve in these areas, and often find that inner sense, simply by developing the right habits.

Thrift is the ability to manage one's money and possessions wisely—in other words: knowing what's worth buying, and what you don't need. It's a quality that often gets shortchanged in our daily lives.

We live in a country where most people love to spend money, and we tend to give more trust than we should, to people who have money to spend.

If there's one thing our society respects, its riches. When we see someone get a new car, or buy a new wardrobe, we interpret these observations as signs that the person is doing well. If we see owning a certain item as a sign that its owner is rich, we often want the same thing for ourselves. That's human nature. Yet, if we were to look at the bank account behind the new car or new wardrobe, we might find that these signs are false, and the account is overdrawn. Thrift is the ability to avoid these kinds of purchases unless we truly need them, or until we can afford to pay for them with our own money.

Some immature individuals take society's respect for riches, and twist it into a sneering disrespect for thrift. They think of being thrifty as the same as being cheap, or small-time. They see people who've developed the habits of saving, and paying on time with cash, and they immediately regard these seemingly slow, dull folks as misers.

These same immature minds often mistake the appearance of wealth for the reality of wealth. They assume the man with many glittering possessions must be their wise and intelligent hero. They see him driving his big, sleek new car (or he might even have a driver), and then watch him ride his private elevator up to a newly furnished penthouse apartment, and they believe everything he tells them about his road to success. When he says he's learned the secret to gaining great wealth, they trust that he's telling the truth. When he says that, for just a little investment, he can make them rich too, they willingly give him their savings. Many of his victims know deep down that his schemes are nothing but con games or drug deals, but they persuade themselves that this one must be an exception… or they believe they can get out in time, before his house-of-cards falls. Or they simply ignore that tiny voice in them that's trying to scream the truth. These are people who have buried their honesty with shovelfuls of desire. Real thrift is built on real honesty.

Some people are thrifty by nature, but even among those who have this talent, the habits that go along with thrift are often hard to develop because of all the media messages that bombard us every day. Advertising, movies, and unending waves of new products encourage us to buy more and more, and to show off our new purchases to everyone around us. The habits of thrift can help us resist these influences.

We should all think of thrift as a constant goal. We reach it by learning the difference between what we want and what we need. Let's take an example where you go into a supermarket to get meat for the next few dinners. In your pocket you have $15. You see chicken for a dollar a pound, and Porterhouse steak for $15 a pound. If you're in the habit of spending whatever it takes to get exactly what you want right now, you'll probably spend all of your cash on a one-pound steak. You'll eat it tonight, and maybe have just enough left over for a sandwich tomorrow. Make sure you cook it just the way you like it, because it's all you'll have for awhile. If you've developed the habit of thrift you'll buy the chicken instead. You buy 15 pounds of it, then, after cooking enough for the next couple of nights, you freeze about 14 pounds. Now you have meat for a month instead of just two nights. That's being thrifty.

On a larger scale, say you're ready to buy a car. A friend of yours is selling his 6-year-old Honda Accord. It's a car you've seen every day since he bought it new. You've ridden in it, and even driven it a couple of times. He's asking $11,000. The price would fit "sensibly" into your budget, and, if you haggle with him a little, you can probably get him to drop it a little. Then there's that Escalade everybody's been ogling on the next block over. A new Escalade will cost close to $70,000, but you think you could just barely meet the monthly payments, and if you're going to be successful, you have to look the part, right? This is a lot like the decision to buy the Porterhouse steak, but its effects will be with you much longer. If you've trained yourself to consistently choose the chicken, it will be easier to decide to buy the Honda. Why? Because you've learned the real value of your money. You automatically bring this knowledge to every purchase you make. If you do this consistently, others will notice. Soon you will see that the respect thrift earns you is greater, and lasts longer, than the respect you would have gotten driving around in that Escalade. And earning this respect actually *saved* you money. That's a habit that's worth the effort.

How do you develop the habits of thrift? By always looking at items in terms of their prices, and your bottom-line needs. You must immunize yourself against the lure of fleeting symbols of wealth, and concentrate your efforts on real, core values. When you see a flashy new car, or someone showing off their new bling-bling, think of these things only in terms of price, and this person's ability to pay. Can he really afford it? At the end of each night does he park his shiny new luxury car in front of a falling down dump of a house?

Once you've answered these questions, you will find that many apparent signs of affluence transform into signs of ignorance and debt. If you find yourself envying this person's wealth, ask yourself: Do you envy the wealth itself, or what he buys with it? Do you want that car? Are you really that envious of the man's bling-bling? Is that the reason you want money? Or do you want to use your money to create a more secure and comfortable life for yourself and your family? If you answer these questions with honesty and objectivity, and if you decide on a future of security, comfort and good things for your family, you are developing the habits of thrift.

Generosity might seem like the opposite of thrift, but often that's an illusion. Some generosity is similar to flashy new cars and bling-bling. The donor writes a big check, or buys an ostentatious gift, but all he really wants is attention. Or he needs to perform an act of atonement. Many bad boys, who've gone on to bigger, more profitable crimes, feel guilty about their ill-gotten gains. They give money to good causes to ease their badly battered consciences. When giving is motivated purely by guilt, that's not real generosity; it's just another failed attempt to buy righteousness.

"Beware of practicing your piety before men in order to be seen by them; for then you will have no reward from your Father in heaven. Thus, when you give alms, sound no trumpet before you, as the hypocrites do in the synagogues and in the streets, that they may be praised by men."

Matthew 6: 1-2

Acts of fake generosity benefit the giver only for as long as his frauds remains hidden. Real generosity provides the giver with the warmth and satisfaction of seeing his wealth at work improving other peoples' lives. Nonetheless, real generosity can be a two-edged sword.

Sometimes a well-meaning young man gets his life back on track, and starts a business. Let's say this young man is you. Your business does well, and for the first time you, the bright new entrepreneur, can see a lot of money coming in. At first you do just fine, using all these profits to pay off old bills, while you sets some money aside in savings. You enjoy these first signs of growing wealth, and you are soon completely caught up in the beginnings of your success. Then the needy charities arrive.

Most of these charities are truly good causes. Some are church-sponsored, while others begin in schools, social clubs, and other organizations. Representatives of the food bank come calling, then, a local summer camp needs funds. They arrive at your business, and see your employees serving new customers, and ringing up sales. They come into your freshly painted office, and sit in a well-upholstered chair on the other side of your executive-style desk. You've created this workplace to inspire yourself and your employees to always reach higher. You've also spent your entire decorating budget for the year.

In a way you've created a vicious circle. Your business has gotten off the ground, and you've had some success. Money is coming in much faster than you expected. You notice that the customers who spend the most are the ones who are most impressed by your rising fortunes. To keep these customers coming, you spend some of your first year's revenue making your place of business look better than ever. All of that makes sense.

Though these improvements to your workplace have the desired effect of inspiring trust in your customers, they also inspire hope in the hearts and offices of your local charities. The only thing the representatives of these charities know about your bottom line is what they see when they arrive at your business. If they see prosperity, they want to get you to give more. That's their job. When they think of your revenues they immediately think of how much of that can be spared for their very good causes. Charities always need every penny they can find. They need money for the sick, lame, ignorant, helpless, and homeless. When they arrive you should give them what you can.

However, when you are just starting your business, and in the months, and possibly years, that it takes you to earn a good profit, you must be careful not to let generosity become a fault. Naturally, you shouldn't give anything you don't really have (never, never donate money using a credit card), nor should you give to impress others.

You should also be careful of that old line: "It's deductable." In that first year your income might be so small that your taxes are almost nothing, making the value of the deduction as low as zero. This is a time to look at these charities, and decide which ones you want to support in years to come. This year your checks will be small—maybe even tiny. If so, you might compensate by finding some way to volunteer hours of time, and provide other cash-less benefits. You can encourage your employees to do the same, possibly setting up a program for volunteerism. Maybe you have a room where a community group could meet. Or perhaps you and your employees can organize a charity benefit such as a softball game, raffle, or a blood drive. This can satisfy your generous urges for a minimum of cash, while also directly benefiting your community.

Two parts of your personal inventory often go together: *alertness,* or your ability to pay attention, and *patience,* which is often nothing more than being able to wait and see what will happen.

These qualities might be most essential when little or nothing is happening. That's when we grow so tired of waiting that we drift off to sleep.

When you start a business, or get a job, perhaps your biggest task is always that of paying attention. Your first concerns are usually basics, such as ordering goods, stocking shelves, organizing employees and their tasks, and making sure customers are always cared for. All of these—and everything else—require you to pay attention. The time factor is inevitable here, but this also involves focus and energy. As Loehr and Schwartz argue in "The Power of Full Engagement": "Energy, not time, is the fundamental currency of high performance." Every business has a million details. There are calls to make, orders to fill, books to keep, services to provide, and customers to cultivate. Someone has to keep an eye on all of these jobs. If you're the boss, you must ensure that someone is covering each one. If you are an employee, you should understand which details are your responsibilities, and always make sure you give them your full attention.

When someone walks into this business, you, or one of your employees should be visible, available, and attentive. Your customer should immediately encounter someone who says: "Hello! May I be of assistance?" It's one of those questions that might seem routine, but train yourself to always listen carefully to the answer. After all, this is your first contact with someone who might become a faithful customer for decades.

Alertness works best when it's accompanied by patience—a quality that helps in almost any endeavor. Learning how to do a job takes time. Learning how to run a business takes longer. You must be patient with yourself, and with others. If it takes a minimum of several weeks or months to get an operating license for your business, you must find the patience to wait. When you open your doors, and wait for the customers to come in, you must accept that this will take time.

Patience is an inner quality, but it can also be learned. The best way to attain it is to follow the same method we applied to objectivity: step back from your desires, and then, instead of (or along with) using this distance to produce objectivity, let it separate you from the object of your impatience. Keep watch on that object, so that you can act when the time comes, but in the meantime return your attention to all those other little details that keep your business running.

Most of us have other things in our personal inventories. You might have a talent for numbers, while I might have the ability to get along with people. A sense of fairness always helps, as do things like focus and a steady temperament. When we understand ourselves, and our inner qualities, that knowledge will help us find the right jobs, or make the right investments of our time and energy. These abilities are at the foundation of all our future success.

QUESTIONS (Check one answer for each):

1. A marathon is unique because:

a. It's route isn't an absolutely straight line.

b. It requires a lot of stamina, but little training.

c. No one is trying to win it.

d. It's so long.

2. Our personal inventory is made up of:

a. Things we keep in our bedrooms ___

b. All of our possessions, wherever we keep them ___

c. The things we want ___

d. Our inner qualities ___

3. The best way to be generous is to:

a. Pick a high-profile charity that will advertise your contribution ___

b. Find a single charity, and encourage thriftiness by giving only a little ___

c. Keep all of your business profits, but encourage your employees to give liberally___

d. Give what you sensibly can, and find opportunities for volunteer work for you and your employees ___

4. Patience is important because:

a. Everything takes too much time, so we must learn to quietly wait no matter what happens ___

b. It's essential to stop worrying, and take some time off ___

c. Speed and timing are overrated ___

d. It gives us a chance to step back, attend to other details, and gain objectivity___

5. What other inner qualities do you have in your personal inventory? How might that benefit you?

_____
_____
_____
_____
_____
_____
_____
_____
_____
_____
_____
_____
_____

6. Are there any qualities that you think you may need? What are they? Why do you need them? How might you acquire them?

_____
_____
_____
_____
_____
_____
_____
_____
_____
_____
_____
_____
_____
_____
_____
_____
_____
_____
_____
_____
_____
_____
_____
_____

Chapter 4

Education, Credit, and Finance

"For whatever was written in former days was written for our instruction, that through endurance and through the encouragement of the Scriptures we might have hope."

Romans 15:4

As we've seen, you can't run life's marathons without preparation. Whether you're applying for a job or starting a business, you have to be ready for all that comes with it. That means you must have whatever education and training you need to do the job you want. Or, if you're starting a small business, "ready" means you have enough cash to cover the first few months' bills and contingencies, and enough credit to serve as a cushion against the rough patches.

How do you get these things? You begin with what you have. In Chapter Three we talked about your personal inventory. If you are honest and alert, and if you are willing to learn to be patient and thrifty, you have the raw materials for success. These are the qualities you bring to the task of turning your life around.

Many of you probably have some education and training. The skills you've developed might not be obvious at first, even to you, but many of us have learned some basic job skills without even knowing it. If you have held a job—almost any job—for a few months, you should be able to identify some talents and abilities that allowed you to keep that job.

This might be something as basic as getting there on time. A famous standup comic once said: "Eighty percent of success is just showing up." He was right. Though the other twenty percent is incredibly important, you can't deal with any of that until you actually get to the workplace. If showing up for work is a challenge you must find ways to motivate yourself. That's not so hard when you like your work, but many entry-level jobs (the kind we usually get when we're just starting out) are repetitive and boring. In such a situation, you should keep your eyes on the prize. If you do your entry-level job well, more interesting and better paying jobs will open up for you.

Two other basic job skills are: listening and processing information. You must develop the ability to concentrate on what others are saying. Once you've heard what the other person is saying, you should be able to understand it, and know the proper response.

At first this might seem simple. The boss points to a stack of boxes on a loading dock, and says: "Load those boxes onto the truck." You follow his instruction, and put the boxes into the truck. But sometimes it gets more complicated.

If you watch a good waiter in a restaurant, you can see how an expert listens, and processes information. The waiter smiles, describes specials, answers questions, and then takes orders. He writes quickly on his order pad, or he might key the data into a handheld device. If the restaurant is full, this waiter will be serving several tables, with two or more diners at each table. Sometimes he'll be taking care of twenty or more customers at a time. A single table could have six or more diners. Each has a particular order, including appetizer, entrée, beverage, and so on. Many items require even more choices, such as how you want your meat cooked, or what you want on your sandwich.

The experienced waiter listens carefully to each person's instructions, writes down the orders correctly, and then conveys all of this information to the kitchen staff. He might have as many as twenty, or even thirty specific instructions from a single table of four. In the kitchen he listens to find out if there will be any problems with these orders. If there are, he must correctly communicate this information to any affected diners. As the cooks put the finished orders out for pickup, the waiter sets them on a tray, takes them to the table, and serves each dish to the person who ordered it. Though, as in any work, there are occasional mistakes, a good waiter gets it right almost every time. As he serves them the meals they've ordered, his regular customers wonder how he does it.

If you've never been a waiter, this kind of work might seem to be as complex as rocket science, but most waiters and waitresses master these basic skills in just a few weeks. How? They train themselves to listen, and process information.

This isn't all that different from the tasks you did as a student in school. A student takes in information from lectures, conversations, video presentations, books, and other sources, and then he shows that he understands that information in class discussions, papers, and tests. But a student has to do more than a waiter. The student has to learn things, and then put them together in different ways. For instance, a business student might learn how restaurants work, and then he might see a way to combine a diner with a laundromat, or a bistro with a grocery store.

All of this training comes under the label of "education." Education is a huge factor in turning your life around. Employers want it, customers ask about it, and we all need it.

An intelligent heart acquires knowledge, and the ear of the wise seeks knowledge.

Proverbs, 18:15

If you're looking for a job, education is almost always an issue they'll ask about. Most employers want people who can read, write, and do some basic math. Many businesses insist that job applicants have some kind of diploma. This might seem like a huge obstacle for a dropout, but if you don't have a diploma, with some preparation you can get one simply by passing a test. Anyone who hasn't graduated from high school should take their state's General Educational Development test, otherwise known as the GED. Those who pass this receive a high school diploma, usually from the state's education department.

Some entry-level jobs don't require a diploma. Some of these are dead-end positions offering nothing but a minimum wage paycheck, but others are a part of training programs. These programs often offer certificates showing that you've successfully completed them. Some certificates don't mean much, but others are better than many diplomas or degrees. They show that you have developed specific skills, so for some jobs certification is even more important than graduation. Of course, if you have a certificate *and* a diploma, that's even better.

If you are starting a business, you might not have to worry about having a diploma, but you should have whatever education is necessary to run your business. For instance, if you want to start a plumbing service, you must be trained as a plumber. You can get this by taking classes, or through on-the-job training. Most plumbers begin as plumbers' apprentices. The successful apprentice learns the skills, passes a test, and gets a journeyman license. As a journeyman, the plumber continues his training, and eventually takes another test. If he passes he becomes a master plumber. Then he can start his own plumbing business. Eventually, through a similar process, he might get a general contractor's license.

Some businesses are much easier to start. Most cities and counties don't have any educational requirements for owning a restaurant. Anyone can do it. If our waiter from the earlier example wants to open his own restaurant, he's free to try. All he needs is financing and plenty of energy. But if his restaurant is going to become a success, he needs more.

We know that our waiter has the skills to get to work, and to listen, and process information. He understands how a restaurant works *from a waiter's point of view.* But does he understand the rest of it?

Let's assume our waiter doesn't have much formal education—not even a high school diploma. We will also assume that he can read and do math just fine. He's been working in restaurants since he was 15 years old. He began as a dishwasher, then worked his way up to prep cook, then line cook. (In most restaurant kitchens, prep cooks prepare ingredients, line cooks do the actual cooking, and chefs direct the whole process.) Our waiter thought of going to cooking school, but decided on waiting tables instead. He's done that in three different restaurants, each with a different style and theme. He's spent some time bartending as well. In his current job he worked several months as the restaurant's manager when the regular manager was recovering from an illness. The restaurant's owner would have kept him in that position if the regular manager hadn't come back to work.

Though our waiter lacks a diploma, he has plenty of training. Not only has he worked in kitchens, on the restaurant floor, and in management, but he's succeeded in all three. His work has always led to good results, and he's consistently moved up the ladder.

If you are at the beginning of this process, with few skills, and not much formal education or training, you might look for an entry-level job in a business that doesn't require new workers to have degrees, diplomas, or certifications. These jobs include work in restaurants, on construction sites, and often in small retail shops and stores. Getting the job is just the start. Once you have it, you need to do it well. You must show up on time, listen to others, and use the information they give you to do the job as well as you possibly can. If you do it well enough, people will begin to notice. Like our waiter, you will earn promotions, and when you are ready you might go into business for yourself.

This is when you need financing, which usually means you need credit. You can start some businesses without much money, but most of these involve certain skills and training. Many cleaning and moving businesses begin with one person doing the work. You have a truck, help a friend move as a favor, and a neighbor hires you to do the same thing for money. You clean out someone's garage, and the guy down the street notices. He hires you to get all the junk out of his basement. This leads to similar work, and before you know it, you're in business.

But most businesses must have financing. Someone has to approach investors or banks, and sell them on the idea that this new business can make real profits. This is when you need credit, which is another way of saying you need credibility. Credibility is the trust that people put in you and what you do. If a ballplayer says he can hit a home run, and he steps up to the plate, and does it, he's established his credibility. The team's owner will gladly pay for that kind of performance. But if the ballplayer makes his claim, then strikes out, his credibility is damaged. Investors and banks look at their borrowers for signs of credibility. The more credible you and your plans are, the more credit they offer. This translates into real loans that can help you start your business.

If you want to approach lenders or investors, you must be ready to show them that you know what you're doing. They want to be sure that you have a sensible plan. One of the best ways to do this is to create a business proposal. This proposal/plan is a little like a paper you would write for school.

There are many kinds of business proposals, and you can find examples of them online. All of them have certain features in common. A proposal should begin with a brief summary what products and/or services the company would provide. It should describe the potential customers, and why they will be willing to pay for the things you are offering. It should outline potential costs and profits, and deal with matters like suppliers, location, parking, and so on.

Our waiter's proposal would begin with the kind of restaurant he wants to open, and where he wants to locate it. If he's dreaming of a Chinese restaurant on a block that already has six of them, he might have a problem, but if he's opening an Italian place, and there's nowhere to get pasta within ten miles, that might be an advantage. He should be specific about his target audience. Do the people in this community already drive twenty miles for Italian food? Or do they prefer Chinese meals? Our waiter must answer these questions, and back up his words with proof. He must figure out rent, utilities, and taxes. He must price tables, chairs, and kitchen appliances. Though some of this won't go into his proposal, he should have the information ready. That way, when he meets with bankers and investors, he has the details right there at his fingertips.

Though formal written proposals are usually used for business start-ups, you can apply the same methods to writing a plan for yourself. It might be put together like this:

1. Overall goals: This should describe where you want to be in five years, then where you hope to be in ten years. What kind of job do you really want? Where do you really want to live? Do you want to marry? Have children? Work at a job you really enjoy? Retire early?

_____
_____
_____
_____
_____
_____
_____
_____
_____
_____

2. Housing: A description of where you live, how much it costs, and what you get for what you pay. If you want to move, this section might also include a description of the kind of place you're looking for, and its potential costs.

_____
_____
_____
_____
_____
_____
_____
_____
_____
_____

3. Transportation: This covers your present transportation methods, and potential upgrades, along with costs and benefits of each.

_____
_____
_____
_____
_____
_____
_____

4. Education and Occupation: List all schooling and training that you already have. Follow this with the job you really want, and then list the educational and training qualifications you need to get it. Write a brief account of how you can get the education and training.

_____
_____
_____
_____
_____
_____
_____
_____
_____
_____
_____
_____
_____
_____

5. Happiness: Write down the things that you need for a happy life. That means you should list whatever you need to feel fulfilled. Do you need a big house? Would you be just as happy in a small apartment? Do you need an expensive car? Or would an inexpensive car be enough? Do you need to get married? Have children? List the things you need the most to become the best man you can be. This can be the summary and conclusion of your plan.

_____
_____
_____
_____
_____
_____
_____
_____

Whether you are starting a business, or simply setting up a sensible plan for your personal finances, the same principles apply: if you want to make money, save money, and finally succeed at piling up real wealth, you must produce enough money to pay your bills, and to save for the future. Your savings might go into the financing of other businesses, but first you must bring home enough money to put some aside.

In business, and in our personal lives, credit is a two-edged sword. It can help us do what we want to do when we want to do it. It can also creep up on us unnoticed, and ruin our lives.

"The rich rule over the poor, and the borrower is the slave of the lender."

Proverbs 22:7

To use credit well, we must understand how it works. "Credit" is trust. If a lender extends credit to you, he is providing you with access to loans, and he trusts you to pay him back with interest.

He might just hand you the money, or the loan might come in the form of a "line of credit." With a line of credit, you don't have to borrow (or pay interest on) the whole amount. You can take what you need, pay interest on that, and the rest stays where it is. You can still get whatever's left without applying for another loan, or you can leave it with the lender. Your lender trusts you to use whatever amount you take in a way that will provide you with enough profits to repay the loan with interest.

If you only use credit when you really need it, and if you keep track of the principle (the amount you borrow) and interest, and if you always seek the lowest interest, you are using credit wisely. If you use this credit to grow your business, and create more profit than the total cost of the loan (principle-plus-interest & fees), then you are using credit wisely. If you are simply using credit to take care of earlier unpaid loans, and if you're not sure how much interest you're paying, or when you'll be out of debt, then you are letting your creditors take all the profits. As long as you keep paying the interest, they'll extend you more and more credit. However, in the end you might go bankrupt, owing them thousands of dollars. They know that's not likely to happen until you've paid so much in interest and fees that they still come out with a profit. Your bankers don't want you to go broke, but they always structure their loans so that they are better prepared than you are for that possibility.

Too many people get caught in the trap of credit. This is particularly true of debt from credit cards. Credit cards are really lines of credit, but they can be far more costly than most bank loans. Most cards start out with low interest rates, but as soon as you've owed them money for a couple of months, those rates begin to skyrocket. Many credit cards charge their holders nearly 30% interest.

Most people who are trying to turn their lives around should avoid credit cards. In today's world this requires discipline, and occasionally other financial choices. Prior to credit cards, young people usually relied on parents or relatives for loans. Sometimes these young people sold their possessions to raise funds. For someone in this position a credit card is tempting.

You can buy things without anyone else knowing that you're borrowing the money to do it. There's no need to explain this to anyone. Your family and friends think you have the money, and see you as being richer than you really are. Your apparent riches often bring you respect from others. But the more you do this, the more difficult it is to stop. It's a vicious cycle that often leads to bankruptcy or worse.

The key to successful finance—whether business or personal—is to create an ongoing process of taking in more money than you spend. You should try to do this every year, every month, and, if possible, every day. If you have a time each month when you pay your bills, that time should also be used for figuring out your total income and your total spending. Your income should always be more than you've spent. If it's not you should know exactly why, and find a solution.

Questions:

1. If you don't have a diploma or a degree, which of the following options should be your goal (pick two):

a. A minimum wage job with no training or benefits, but with a weekly paycheck.

b. Passing the GED exam.

c. A minimum wage job with lots of overtime.

d. A job where you can get on-site training and certifications.

2. The best ways to establish your credibility are (pick two):

a. Talking about all the things you've done, and exaggerating your qualifications.

b. Doing your job honestly and well.

c. Earning certifications, diplomas, and other credentials.

d. Getting your best friend to vouch for you.

3. Why should you avoid using credit cards to finance a business? (Pick one)

a. Because it's easy to lose your credit card, and it's hard to get a new one.

b. Because using a credit card makes you a target for identity thieves.

c. Because credit cards make it too easy to go deeply into debt without really noticing.

Chapter 5

Becoming Mr. Perfect:

Understanding the role of the man in the family and community

Blessed is the man who walks not in the counsel of the wicked, nor stands in the way of sinners, nor sits in the seat of scoffers; but his delight is in the law of the Lord, and on his law he meditates day and night. He is like a tree planted by streams of water that yields its fruit in its season, and its leaf does not wither. In all that he does, he prospers.

Psalms 1, 1-4

Who is the perfect man, and what makes him perfect? Philosophers have puzzled over this for thousands of years. Just about all of them agree that he must be strong, honest, and courageous, but how are these qualities supposed to operate in real life situations? Perfection isn't possible, but if you have a clear idea of what a perfect man *should be*, you can better understand the goal you are seeking, and find ways to get ever-closer to your target.

The perfect man must be strong. Just about everyone agrees on this, but what do we mean by "strong?" When we hear that word, most of us immediately imagine physical strength. Boxers are known for this, as are football players and weight lifters, but seeing strength purely in terms of knockouts, tackles, or bench pressing numbers misses the real meaning.

Physical strength is a helpful quality that sometimes becomes a necessity. You want this kind of strength whenever you have to move a refrigerator, stove, or piano. You also want it when you have to fight your way out of a corner. But what if you were born with genes that make you five-foot-five and 110 pounds? What if a car crash leaves you permanently crippled? What if your body just isn't as strong as an NFL lineman's—or that of a man who moves refrigerators?

Physical strength isn't everything, but it certainly helps. All of us have some strength, even if it's only enough to open one's eyes. Whatever your level of physical strength, you can do things to increase it. You can workout, doing exercises that will make your body as strong and toned as it can possibly be (see Chapter 6). In addition, you may learn to use tools, equipment, and methods that make up for your weakness. Doing these things is usually smart. When we are stronger and more able, we are also healthier, which brings us closer to being the best that we can be.

But all the physical strength in the world won't make you Mr. Perfect. It doesn't even guarantee that you'll win in a physical confrontation. After all, David was no physical match for Goliath, but the young boy stopped the giant with a single stone from his slingshot. Might doesn't always mean right.

If you're trying to become Mr. Perfect, you need a different kind of strength. You need the inner toughness to do what's right, even when it would be easier to do wrong, or do nothing. This kind of strength gives you the focus you need to see a situation clearly and objectively. This inner strength is closely connected to conscience— the ability to tell right from wrong.

The weak man is constantly tempted, and usually gives in. Thus, he's not only weak; he's not to be trusted. If he's married, he gives in to the lure of other women. If he's broke he gives in to his urge to steal. If he goes into business, his customers must be careful when using his products and services. They can't entirely trust his work because he always does just enough to get by. When something goes wrong, he dodges all blame, often lying to avoid responsibility.

Mr. Perfect's strength is in his character. He does whatever needs to be done. When the going gets tough, he protects his turf. He's capable of defending his home and family. This doesn't mean he's capable of going toe-to-toe with a champion heavyweight boxer. It means that he can foresee most trouble and remain calm enough to create the best defense possible.

A weak-spirited man who's trying to protect his home and family might buy a gun. The clerk at the gun shop shows him how to load it and take off the safety. Having mastered these skills, the weak man is convinced that he knows how to use the gun. After all, it can't be that hard to point the thing and shoot. Right? He's seen them do it on TV a million times. With a gun, the weak man feels that he can be a real man. He assumes this will make him a better husband and father. He believes that might makes right. Many weak people believe this until something happens that shows them the truth.

This normally weak and timid husband and father comes home, and puts the gun in his nightstand drawer. Its presence there gives him a strong sense of false confidence. If something bad happens, he thinks he can handle it. He's seen other men do it on TV and in a thousand movies. Then, when his wife wakes him from a sound sleep, saying she hears an intruder downstairs, he grabs his loaded gun, goes out to the upstairs hall, and takes aim at the threatening shadow below. He yells something, but the shadow doesn't answer right away. Before this suddenly "strong" man knows what's happened, he's pulled the trigger, and the "intruder" lies dead at the foot of the stairs. It's their teenaged son. The weak man's attempt to protect his home has brought him nothing but tragedy.

The man with real inner strength might buy the gun, but the rest of the story would be different. If this strong man knew nothing about guns, he would ask the man behind the counter about courses covering the proper handling and care of firearms. He would read articles and statistics, and he would study the uses, limits and dangers of guns. He would learn to clean the gun, and keep it locked up where his children can't get to it.

When the truly strong man's son comes home late from a date, the man doesn't automatically reach for a loaded gun. He might make sure it's there, but he doesn't have his finger trembling on a hair trigger. Instead this man goes out in the hall, and calls down the stairs: "Who's there?" When he hears a garbled voice, he doesn't automatically regard it as a threat. When he realizes he's hearing his son's familiar reply: "It's me, Dad," any thoughts he might have had about the gun fade away. The gun stays in its drawer.

The father goes down the stairs, and asks his son if he wants to share in a midnight snack with his dad. His strength has assured that these two can share this moment together. The gun is for emergencies. A man with courage doesn't fear every sound, and learns to separate nighttime shadows from real threats.

It's easier for the truly strong man to have courage. That's because he starts out with another, related quality: honesty. This is a man who's truthful. He's made a lifelong habit of evaluating situations as fully as possible, then saying what he really thinks. He doesn't play games, or deceive others, or withhold vital information. This stand-up guy doesn't call attention to the fact that he's telling the truth. He simply says what he has to say. He's honest and upright, but he never makes any big deal about it. When the subjects of honor and integrity come up, he makes no claims, but allows others to judge for themselves. If his character is questioned he puts the questions to rest with honest words and actions. He doesn't need to advertise himself. Instead, his honesty and integrity are a lot like breathing: they are such basic parts of his makeup that people seldom even notice they are there. Yet, without even knowing it, they depend on those qualities because they depend on this man.

Strength is also the key to endurance. A strong man can withstand a lot of emotional punishment. If he loses a friend or family member, the strong man grieves, and perhaps he even breaks down in tears, but he never loses his core strength. He understands his world has changed. He knows he has lost something vital that might never be replaced. Yet he also has no doubt that he will endure this pain, and go on to live his life. When a strong man's family suffers a loss, he stands, like a pillar, supporting them. They know he will be there to lean on. He will share in all of their grief, but when all is said and done, he will endure the tragedy, inspiring all of those around him.

Do you see a man skillful in his work? He will stand before kings.

Proverbs 22:29

A truly strong man will take pride in his home and his work. This is not the same as the sinful pride we often see in others and ourselves. Pride is a sin when it is motivated by selfishness, greed, and egotism. When we are proud because we think we are better than others, that is the sin of pride. The same is true when our pride leads us to boast that we have what others want.

A strong, courageous man's pride is not in his superiority or his possessions. Gaining social status, or buying a new car, won't make him proud. The man with real strength of character takes pride in his home and his work because they are his own real accomplishments. President Obama takes pride in his two terms in the White House because of the things he's done while in office. While facing huge obstacles, he has served his country, helping to make the world a more peaceful and prosperous place for all of us.

Martin Luther King and Malcolm X could both take pride in their work. Both men gave everything they had to the cause of civil rights. Using different styles and tactics, both of these leaders pushed ahead, creating the pressure that forced America to change for the better. They wanted to do the best work possible, and they did. One of their admirers, Spike Lee, is careful about the kind of work he accepts. Responding to questions about projects people bring to him, the film director says: "I get offers to do something where the money's nice, but it's not something I want to do." He only works on projects he believes in. That's the mark of a man who has strength and courage, and is secure in himself.

All of these are good examples of men who have made a place for themselves in the larger community around them. They've done it by committing themselves to the accomplishment of essential tasks, and then they followed through on that commitment. In doing these things, these men changed history, and made all of our lives better.

A strong man might work for himself, or for an employer or boss. He might own his own home, or rent the most modest apartment. He might have a big family, or he might be single. There are things he doesn't have: fear, greed, spitefulness and disloyalty.

He's learned to avoid these things by finding and developing his qualities of personal strength.

If he works for others, this man provides honest labor. When he says he's going to show up on time, he does. When he gets to work, he gives a hundred percent, earning every penny of his paycheck. If this man starts his own business, his customers and employees soon learn that they are dealing with an honest entrepreneur. He never makes excuses, and his only pride is in providing a quality product, and doing the job well.

"Man, alone, has the power to transform his thoughts into physical reality; man alone can dream, and make his dreams come true."

Napoleon Hill

No man is "Mr. Perfect." Perfection is impossible in any human being. But all of us should think of perfection as our goal. Perfection is an ideal. Mr. Perfect is the image of an ideal we should all pursue. The fact that we can't quite reach it is just one more reason to try. Each time we try, we come a little closer to our ideal. As Mr. Hill said, we can make our dreams come true, but he could have added that we must be prepared to see them adapt to changing circumstances. When we adapt our perfect dreams to reality, our imperfect world is bound to improve a little.

A strong, courageous man is not rigid in his attitudes. He can forgive the sins of others, and understand the imperfections in himself. He is precise, focused, and demanding of those who work with him, but he is also willing to extend patience and charity to those in need. He does his job to the best of his ability, then returns home, and becomes as good a husband and father as he can be.

Questions:

Which of the following is true:

1. Every man who has inner strength and courage can lift 500 pounds. ____

2. No man is perfect. ____

3. Every man knows how to handle a gun properly and safely. ____

4. The only way a man can find courage is to start a business. ____

5. A man who works for a boss doesn't need to be a man. His boss will protect him. ____

6. A real man gives 50% on the job, and 50% at home. ____

7. Courage and honesty are not related to one another. ____

Chapter 6

Healthy and Sexy:

Working Out and Eating Right

"Don't you realize that your body is the temple of the Holy Spirit, who lives in you and was given to you by God? You do not belong to yourself, for God bought you with a high price. So you must honor God with your body."

1 Corinthians 6: 19-20

Physical strength doesn't define manhood, but a man who doesn't keep up his body has a much harder time maintaining the health of his mind and soul. The better your body works, the less worry your mind has. The less worried you are in your mind, the more at peace you will be in your soul.

To reach your peak of physical strength you must get yourself into the best shape possible. The tools for this task are diet and physical workouts. Diet is obvious; whatever you put into your body will affect your health and strength. Working out is a basic the building block in any program to improve the functions of your mind and body. It builds mental focus and stamina. Though many men do it just because they want to look good, the more lasting effects of a long-term workout plan are a body that feels good, and an ability to be more productive in everything you do.

The desire to be strong and fit exists in just about everybody, but young men feel it more intensely than any other group. If you don't believe me, look at the world of sports. In this country we pay more attention to male athletes between the ages of 18 and 35 than any other group. These are the years when most athletes are at their best. Though women are competing in sports more and more, most of the most famous athletes are still young males. More than 90% of college and professional football, basketball and baseball players are in this age range. Right now these men include LeBron James, Robert Griffin III, Andrew Luck, and most of the other recognizable sports stars of our times. An athlete who's still in his prime when he reaches 40 is a rare thing. There are always a few of them playing in any popular sport, but we notice them because they're so different. Because there are so few of them, we celebrate these aging veterans, but when we watch a great athlete who's 25 or 30 we assume he's performing at his peak.

Young males want to stay in shape for another reason: all those young women out there. A woman wants a man who's strong and fit. She wants him to be able to push the car off the ice slick, or carry that new air conditioner into the house. She wants him to defend her, or even scare off any potential attackers just by looking like he can take them. She wants him to give one kid a ride, while carrying another in his arms. She wants him to be in shape for work, play, love and family. Some women may fall for tubby, weak guys, but most women want physical strength in a man.

"I can do all things through Christ which strengthen me."

Philippians 4:13

Physical strength starts with diet, but also requires some kind of dedicated exercise regimen. The two should be connected. The food you eat should help you build the muscles, and maintain the energy and stamina necessary to fuel your workouts.

The first thing you should do is adjust your thinking. Most of us tend to think of diet and fitness programs the same way we think about a difficult course in school. When we have to take a hard course, we go to class, read the books, and cram as much data as we possibly can into our heads. Often we try to learn all the material as late in the game as possible. That way it's still fresh in our minds when we take the test. On the day of the test, we go in, and show our teacher all the knowledge we've stuffed into our heads. If we pass, it's over. We forget most of what we "learned," and never think about that subject again. Why should we? No one's asking about it, and no one expects us to know about it.

We often see diets and workout programs the same way. We go on a crash diet, lose fifteen pounds, then go right back to stuffing our faces. In a month or two all the pounds are back and we're adding more. So next we start going to the exercise room at the community center. There they offer a course in fitness. We learn all the various exercises, do them religiously for six weeks, return to the diet, eating only the right foods in the right proportions, and the pounds go away again. We finish the course, stick with the program for another six weeks, then we start cheating on the diet and missing some workouts. This time it takes six months to gain back the weight, but because it's so gradual, we don't notice. Within another six months we add another big dose of flab, then we repeat the process.

That's because we see these solutions as quick fixes for a minor problem. We're wrong about both. Though a little extra weight, or a rundown physique might not seem like long-term threats, they are. If we allow ourselves to stay this way, any change will become harder and harder. We'll wind up being obese at 40, with the beginnings of diabetes, heart disease, or some other serious condition. The only solution is to permanently change the way we think about diet and fitness.

That means we have to accept the fact that extra weight is always a problem. Only then can we think realistically about permanent solutions. Rather than going on a reducing diet that will strip off excess weight in a few weeks, find a diet that you can live with, and even enjoy, for the rest of your life. If you're carrying around a whole lot of fat, it might take six months or longer to reach your target weight, but if you do it right, you will stay at that weight, while enjoying your meals more.

The first months of any fitness program are difficult. This is because you're adapting your behavior—never an easy thing to do.

But eventually the diet becomes a habit, and you've achieved a permanent change. Then comes a different problem. You're doing fine with the food, but you you're still ten pounds above your target, and you're only losing about a pound every two weeks.

This is because a permanent diet is the amount you're supposed to be eating to stay at your target weight. If you're 225 pounds at the start, and your target weight is 195, this permanent diet will help you get down to 205 within a couple of months. But losing those last ten pounds will take a lot longer. If you're eating enough to support 195 pounds, that's only a little less than the amount that would maintain 205. But if you've made the diet into a habit, that makes it easier. By this time you've adjusted your expectations to include less food. As you reach your target weight, the only change is that you stop losing weight. Everything else stays the same.

This can also be true with workouts. Some programs want you to build yourself up to the point where you spend most of your free hours exercising. Maybe you have enough free time to do that, but if you don't, look for a program where you build yourself up to the particular goal, then level off. If you don't want to work out for more than an hour a day, five days a week, that should be plenty. But whenever you reach your physical goals, you should already be doing the workouts that you will follow for the foreseeable future.

So you need to stop thinking about these as temporary limitations on your usual lifestyle. Your workout and diet programs should be pretty close to the programs you'll be following permanently. That's why you should have a workout program you can look forward to every day. And that is why your diet should be sensible, but full of tasty meals that are also healthy.

Dieting:

I'm not going to write a cookbook here, nor will I tell you which of the thousands of dieting programs you should follow, but there are a few basics that you should understand. First you must realize that dieting begins in the mind. Its most direct effects are on our bodies, but before we can slim down, pump up, or simply improve our health, we have to find the right diet to support our efforts.

All diets have the same basic ingredients: protein, carb (short for "carbohydrate"), and fat. Within these compounds we find sugars, vitamins, and other life-supporting substances.

Protein is the most plentiful single thing in our bodies. It is the primary ingredient in blood, bones, and all of our most vital organs. Protein builds your muscles, and you burn it to give you energy. A lot of the protein you don't burn ends up right out where we can see it. When you see a full head of hair, you are looking at pure protein. The same is true when you look at fingernails. If you build up your abs and biceps, that's protein you see in the mirror. It's your eyelashes, eyebrows, and even your eyes. Your skin is protein, and so are your liver, heart and lungs. You need enough protein to maintain all of these things because they constantly lose old dead cells that are made up of protein. The cells that replace them are protein too. Protein is also the main ingredient in muscles. But once all these basic bodily needs are met, the rest of the protein you eat is excess. Some excess protein passes through our bodies, but the rest usually turns to fat.

Most food labels list only how much protein is in a serving. Be careful about that. Though a food may have a lot of protein, it might not be the kind that humans can use. Proteins in vegetables are incomplete, and, in many cases, we only get about half as much benefit from them. We can use over 3/4s of the protein in most meats, and even more in milk, cheeses, and eggs. (We can use 94% of the protein in eggs, making them the most efficient protein source in the human diet.) That's why eggs, meats, fish, soybeans, and dairy products not only have the most protein, but theirs is the highest quality. Those people who choose to go vegan, and never eat meat, must find other protein sources. Strict vegans avoid all animal products, which leaves them only nuts, legumes, and certain vegetables. You can build up your body without animal products, but it does make the process more complicated.

Carbs contain sugars that will give you energy over the long haul. This can replace the energy made from protein, allowing your body to use that protein to build more bone and muscle, and maintain vital organs. Carbs also help us regulate our metabolism, providing stability, and back-up nutrients whenever they are necessary. When someone says, "I'm getting a second wind," that's often the carbs he ate for lunch kicking in.

The most popular carbs are pasta, potatoes, rice, bread, and cereal. Most of these foods don't have that much fat, or even that many calories. People who eat these and gain a lot of weight are usually adding sauces, butter, or other fat-and-sugar-filled toppings. Too many carbohydrates seem to go perfectly with foods that load on the pounds.

Some people have bodies that burn carbs off quickly. These are those maddening folks who can eat almost anything and stay slim. But most of us need to limit our intake of carbs. Our bodies don't burn them that quickly, and the unused carbs soon convert to fat.

Fat is a whole lot of calories caught in a jello-like medium. At its best it provides the body with extra calories whenever they are needed. It also acts as a carrier, delivering vitamins and other nutrients from one part of the body to another. Fat keeps our skin from getting rough and dry. Deposits of fat protect many of our vital organs, including the heart. A layer of fat just below the skin helps us hold onto our body heat, insulating us from wintery temperatures. Though fat does all of these things, it is also the most troublesome of the three primary nutrients.

We live in a culture that goes overboard on fat. Most meats, milk products, eggs, and desserts are loaded with fat. Butter and vegetable oils are entirely fat. As if this weren't enough, there are all those excess proteins and carbs. Whatever doesn't burn turns to fat.

Most young male athletes do best with about 10% to 12% body fat. If you simply want to be fit, 15% is fine. When you get up to 20%, you are probably putting on a few extra pounds. America's young males average well above 20%. Most young males should adjust their diets, and exercise a lot more than they do.

"Don't you realize that in a race everyone runs, but only one person gets the prize? So run to win! All athletes are disciplined in their training. They do it to win a prize that will fade away, but we do it for an eternal prize."

                              1 Corinthians 9:24-25

All of the foods I've mentioned here contain various kinds of sugar. The names of most sugars end in *"ose"*. These include sucrose, which is the chemical name for table sugar, fructose, which usually comes from fruits and grains (corn is the biggest commercial source), and glucose, which is found in starches, plants, and animals. Many of today's processed foods are loaded with these sugars. Food producers add them as preservatives, and as sweeteners. Most of us eat far more of these sugars than our bodies need. As is true of any sugar, if we eat too much of it, the body turns it into fat.

Exercise can help you reduce the fat in your body, but it can only do so much. Most reducing diet / exercise programs depend on dieting for weight loss. If you don't reduce your intake of excess fat and sugar, you can exercise during every waking hour, but still gain weight. Yet exercise is still as essential as it ever was. The right exercise program makes sure the weight that's still there is distributed properly. It replaces pounds of fat with pounds of muscle.

Where that muscle goes depends on your exercise program. Runners tend to have lean bodies, and powerful muscles in their legs. Swimmers often have more evenly distributed muscles than any other athletes because powering through water requires about the same level of effort from almost every part of the body. Weight lifting usually builds up shoulders, arms, chest, abdomen, and legs.

Someone who begins dieting and lifting weights at the same time might look in his mirror and see the body he wants. *"That's great"*, he thinks, *"this diet and workout program did exactly what I expected"*. Then the guy follows up by stepping on his bathroom scale. *"What's this?"* he wonders, as confusion and disappointment cloud his mind. The scale says he's only managed to lose a couple of pounds. *"How could that be?"* he asks himself. That's easy. The dieting reduced the fat in his body, while lifting weights added pounds of muscle. The results of these two processes cancel each other out, so when this guy looks at the scale, there's no change. Yet that body he sees in the mirror seems entirely new. Though he might be about the same weight that he was before, he's become much stronger— healthier too.

"For the moment all discipline seems painful rather than pleasant, but later it yields the peaceful fruit of righteousness to those who have been trained by it."
Hebrews 12:11

Workouts:

If you want to go beyond exercise that merely keeps you in shape, you will need to start a real workout program. This is aimed at building muscle, and increasing certain kinds of strength. It is the beginning of bodybuilding.

If you look online, you will see that there are many bodybuilding programs. I'm not going to go into detail about particular bodybuilding methods, but all of the most successful ones are based on a few basic principles. Every bodybuilder has his own way to express these principles, but the steps are almost always similar to these:

1. *Establish your goals.* Look at yourself in the mirror. What do you see that you like? What do you see that you don't like? Is there so much fat on your torso that everything bounces? Does the flesh on your arms flap when you move them? Does your belly look like you must have just eaten two gallons of ice cream? Do you have a double or triple chin? Or maybe you don't have a single ounce of flab.

Maybe you're as skinny as a rail. If you're fat, you want to lose your flab, shedding some, and transforming the rest into toned, buff muscle. If you're rail thin, you want to grow some muscle. You might want to achieve the classic build of a professional weight lifter. Or you might want to develop the lean body of a runner or swimmer. Take whatever you're imagining, and set that as your goal. If it's bigger, better abs, write that down. If you want a flat belly, write that. Put it all down on paper: how you want to look, what needs to go, what needs to stay, and what you want to add to your physique.

2. *Make sure you have the raw material for working out.* The "raw material" of any program is the material that goes into the result. For instance, if you're grilling burgers for your cookout, ground beef, buns, and cheese, etc. are all your raw materials. The cooked burger on a bun on a plate is your final product. If you're building a car, you need steel, plastic, glass, and a few other basics, and the car is your final product. Building your body is no different. Your most basic raw materials are your flesh and bones. The other raw materials are the foods and liquids that go into your body. Every workout program will need a lot of protein to give you energy, and to build all those muscles. Many runners and swimmers want plenty of carbs, while weightlifters usually cut their intake of these, replacing them with even more protein. If your workout program has a diet that goes with it, the foods are usually selected to complement the exercises.

3. *Start slow.* You can't just fast-forward to the exercises for Day 31, and expect your body to follow. This begins with baby steps. Most programs start with the lighter weights, and less strenuous exercises. If you're out of shape, and you lift a hundred pounds ten times, then run five miles on the first day, you'll do yourself more a lot more harm than good. This can go beyond simple stiffness and wind up turning into real physical damage. That's why most fitness programs include separate days for cardio exercises, as well as rest days when you don't work out at all. Anything described by the word "cardio" involves the heart and lungs.

4. *Alternate exercises.* One way to avoid stiffness or worse is to alternate the exercises you do. Most workout programs recognize this principle, and use it in their designs.

If you exercise all of your muscles every day they never have a chance to rest up, and recover from the stress you've put them through. In any muscle-building or toning program, you exercise muscles to a point where they are stressed, but not really hurt. If you do this regularly, but with regular breaks, for weeks, the muscle adapts to the stress by growing bigger and stronger. Soon you must exercise the muscle even further to reach its stress point. You then repeat the process.

Most programs alternate muscle-building days with cardio days. Muscle-building usually involves curls, rollouts, bench presses, dead lifts, squats, and so on. Cardio exercises include treadmill, rowing machine, running, or even just walking.

5. *Rest days.* Many programs also have one or two days per week when you rest. This doesn't mean you take off work or school. You are resting by not working out at all on these days. This rests the whole body, helping you avoid fatigue and injury. The idea of "rest days" is a part of the principle of alternating.

6. *Adaptation.* There is no one-size-fits-all exercise and diet program. We are all different, so each of us will learn to adapt these programs to our individual needs. You might want more cardio in yours, while I might be more concerned with muscle toning. You might emphasize fruits and vegetables in your diet, while I do better on lean meats. That doesn't mean you can break all the rules. It simply means that you can make small changes if necessary.

      Here's the outline of a typical exercise schedule for building yourself up, and keeping yourself strong and fit. Because it doesn't break down neatly into single weeks, I have listed a 15-day schedule. You can start on any day, and then just keep to the schedule. Each workout covers a different set of muscles. I will also give an example of a workout from my personal trainer. Following the workouts, I will tell you some of the foods that go well with this kind of strength-building regimen:

Typical Workout:

    Sunday:
    Workout A: Squats or leg presses, bench press, T-bar row, etc.
    Monday: Rest
    Tuesday: Cardio: Bicycling, treadmill, running, etc.
    Wednesday: Workout B: Dead lifts, pull-ups, push press, etc.
    Thursday: Rest
    Friday: Cardio
    Saturday: Workout A
    Sunday: Rest
    Monday: Cardio
    Tuesday: Workout B
    Wednesday: Rest
    Thursday: Cardio
    Friday: Workout A
    Saturday: Rest
    Sunday: Cardio

Example from my personal trainer:

<u>Ladders & Curls</u>
1. 24 Hamstring Curls (40 lbs)
    a. 100 Arm Curls
    b. 25 Crunches
    c. 400 ft. Jacobs Ladder
2. 50 Hamstring Curls
    a. 75 Arm Curls
    b. 50 Crunches
    c. 300 ft. Jacobs Ladder
3. 75 Hamstring Curls
    a. 50 Arm Curls
    b. 75 Crunches
    c. 200 ft. Jacobs Ladder
4. 100 Hamstring Curls
    a. 25 Arm Curls
    b. 100 Crunches
    c. 100 ft. Jacobs Ladder

How Diet Affects Workouts and vice-versa:

Working out builds muscle, but only if the building materials are already there. This is where diet comes in. There are plenty of diets out there, coming from all different philosophies, and often pursuing different goals. Some of these differences make sense. A defensive lineman will have different needs than a pregnant mother. But building muscle always involves high quality protein sources, so your diet should feature those.

Most bodybuilders want plenty of protein and very little fat, but some don't pay enough attention to vitamins and minerals. These might be thought of as a kind of ignition and distribution system for other nutrients. Many, such as vitamin C, are fat-soluble, so if you take them without some fat in your stomach, they'll pass right through your system. Don't take that as a license to eat a quart of ice cream whenever you take a vitamin, but it does mean those vitamins belong in meals with a little fat in them. Even a lean burger, or a tiny dab of butter on bread will do.

Steak and lean ground beef are excellent muscle-builders. Fish is great too. So are eggs. If you want virtually fat-free eggs, take out the yolks before you cook them. Milk, yogurt, cheeses, and other dairy products are all full of high-quality protein. Once again, be aware of the fat factor. If you want less, get skim milk, or cheese and yogurt made from skim milk. Tofu, and other soybean-based foods are popular among vegans, and those who want to limit their intake of animal products.

If you aren't a bodybuilder, but you are athletic, you might not want so much protein. Most bicyclists, and many runners and swimmers want some protein, but they are also into carbs. They like most styles of potatoes, pastas, grains, and other carb sources. Olympic swimmer, Michael Phelps is famous for his incredibly huge breakfasts. They feature tall stacks of pancakes, large servings of grits, French toast, and several egg sandwiches, with lots of fruit juice to wash it all down. Of course, Phelps spends many hours in the pool every day, often swimming faster than anyone else on earth. That burns up a few calories.

Whatever your dieting goals, don't forget the fruits and vegetables. Oranges, apples, bananas, grapes... eat whatever fruits you like. Use them as deserts, or part of the meal. Mix them up into salads. Then there are vegetables. Many of the most nutritious ones are also rich in color. Greens, like spinach, broccoli, green beans, and lettuce are full of nutrients we need. Carrots, squash and tomatoes have all kinds of vitamins, minerals, and natural sugars.

A lot of it goes back to the advice mothers give their children: eat a balanced diet every day. If you work out too, and avoid alcohol and drugs, a good diet / workout program should help you achieve the best possible health.

Questions:

1. True of false: The best way to diet is to stop eating anything. ____

2. Check the best nutrient for building muscles: carbs ___ protein___ vitamin C___

3. Should bodybuilders do the same exercises every day? Every week? Or on alternate days? _____

4. True or false: Cardio exercise is mainly to improve leg and arm functions. ____

5. Check the kind of nutrients that provide the most sugars: proteins___ carbs___ fat___

6. What bad health habits do you have? What can you do to change that?

_____
_____
_____
_____
_____
_____
_____
_____
_____
_____
_____
_____
_____
_____

7. What are your health goals? How can you best achieve them?

___

Chapter 7

Walk Like an Egyptian:

Paying It Forward

"He who has a bountiful eye will be blessed, for he shares his bread with the poor."

Proverbs: 22:9

In Chapter Three I advised any young entrepreneur to be careful about donating too much money to charities at the moment when a business shows its first signs of success. The concern about this is real, but you shouldn't take it as an excuse to avoid giving. The idea of giving back to your community should be a part of your motivation to succeed from Day One. Before you make any real money—and after that—volunteering is a way to give even more directly.

When you're not yet ready to contribute large sums, spare whatever hours you can for working with the needy. Encourage your staffers and coworkers to do the same. Whenever possible, coordinate your efforts with theirs, multiplying the effects of your good works. This is a healthy first step in paying it forward.

When a man succeeds at his job, or in his business, he should realize that a real man always pays it forward. This means that he uses his success to give others a helping hand. Though donating money to worthy causes is a part of paying it forward, the idea isn't just to write a check or buy a few raffle tickets at the church fair.

Paying it forward is like paying a debt, but you reverse the act. You know that some people have done you good turns through the years, so now, to settle the debt, you do good deeds for others. These aren't things you do for gain, or to feel proud of yourself. You do it because you owe something. So you give your time, energy, and /or money to help those who are as needy (or more needy) than you were. Instead of paying someone back, you're paying forward. That means you're investing your money, time and energy in the community that invested in you.

* * *

As you read this you might be wondering: *When did my community invest in me?* You don't recall getting a check signed by your community, nor do you remember any community helping you out at the bank when you needed a loan. If these are your thoughts, you're forgetting what your community is.

Maybe you understand that your community is the world just outside your door. Maybe your business is in a shopping mall, or in an urban shopping area. Or you might have a business in an office. Maybe your operation requires a large space in a location that's far from everything. When you look out beyond the parking lot there are no houses, or other structures, within miles. But if you are doing something people pay for, you are in a community, and you benefit from it. That would be true even if your business were on the Moon.

The community of almost any business starts with two groups: the people and companies who supply you, and the customers who buy from you. If you've succeeded, all of these people have helped you. If you've opened a convenience store, every child who's bought a candy bar has supported you, and helped you to succeed. If your business is auto repair, the car owners who pay you, and the ones who supply your parts, have helped you succeed.

But your community is wider than that. You have public streets that lead to your business, with sidewalks, traffic lights, and road repair crews to patch the potholes. Those streets are lined with businesses and homes. People own and work in those businesses. Families live in those homes. Among them are your customers. The families live there because there are many different businesses nearby providing them with jobs and the things they want and need. The businesses are there to serve them for a profit.

Your community is also your churches. Though you may or may not be active in religious services, you should pay attention to what goes on in these places of worship. Every church houses a community within the larger community outside its doors. These people are united by faith, but most churches also encourage their membership to contribute to that world outside.

One of the most important parts of your community is its schools. Virtually every town and neighborhood has at least one elementary school, and most have middle schools and high schools as well. Some communities have adult education programs in their classrooms. Like churches, all of these schools are communities within communities.

There are private schools, church-sponsored schools, and, of course, our public schools. Some communities have colleges and universities. In all of these schools we educate our children, getting them to read, write, and do math, while they also learn essential lessons about living with each other. As they get into higher grades they learn more specialized subjects and skills. Eventually this schooling pays off, as educated citizens use their knowledge to build a better community. This is one example of how paying it forward works.

When you succeed, how will you pay it forward? This is something you should think about from the moment you start your efforts to improve yourself. In those early stages, when you're just beginning to put your life together, you're benefiting from all those people who've paid it forward before you. You're taking advantage of training programs, educational opportunities, or programs that help small businesses. You might use a government or church-sponsored resource to get a grant, or a low-interest loan. Or you might benefit from a private charity that brings successful business people together with aspiring entrepreneurs.

These successful folks give their time, effort and money to help you. That gives you an obligation to do the same. All those people are *giving*. They don't expect repayment or profits. Their schools, churches, and community agencies have helped them get where they are. Now they work with those institutions to help others—people just like you. They aren't asking to get anything for their efforts. Most of them would refuse payment you offered. The only way to pay back their generosity is to do what they've been doing: step up, and take your place among those who make up the best part of your community: those who give something of themselves along with their cash contributions.

If you do have money to give, that's no reason to neglect your volunteer efforts. Use your money to fund causes that you really care about. Maybe a special teacher at your grade school helped you along when you were first learning to read and write. She left you with the lifelong habit of reading books. Now she's retired, but she's spending her evenings teaching in an adult literacy program. Call her and ask what the program needs. Don't just contribute money for books and reading devices—see which ones they want, coordinate with the program leaders, and go get these materials yourself. See if there are other things you can *do* to help this program.

* * *

Paying it forward completes the true cycle of success. It begins with your need to turn your life around, and make something better of yourself. It continues with your first efforts at self-improvement. From that point forward the community plays a role. Your efforts to do better begin within yourself, but they mean nothing if they don't affect others. When you learn a skill, or go back to school, or get a job, or start a business, you are working with other people. You're dependent on them, just as they are dependent on you. This is how a community works. It's also why paying it forward is so important.

The cycle continues as your self-improvement efforts pay off. You get the job you want, or your business starts showing real profits. This is when it becomes your turn to give—which is really your turn to pay it forward.

Help other develop healthy minds and bodies. Invest in the good ideas of young, at-risk entrepreneurs. Take an active role in their efforts. Teach disadvantaged young men how to keep in shape. Coach a team that plays your favorite sport. Learn your Bible, and become a Sunday school teacher at your church. Though some might sneer at this, remember: it takes a real man to teach young children the difference between right and wrong.

If you get promotions that come with raises that make you rich, or if your business makes more money than you ever dreamed of, your community will expand. It will include more clients, colleagues and partners from a much broader area. As your community widens, so does the scope of its problems. Don't shy away from this. It's an opportunity. Now you can pay it forward on a broader level, helping more people than ever before. That's only right. If you're part of a much larger community, then that community is supporting you in efforts to gain greater profits and prosperity. It's a debt that never ends.

There's no reason why it should. The debt we owe to our communities is one we will always be paying forward. It's the price of success, and a real man is happy to pay it every day.

Questions:

1. How has your community affected you?

_____
_____
_____
_____
_____
_____
_____

2. How does it benefit you to pay it forward?

_____
_____
_____
_____
_____
_____
_____

3. How do those around you benefit when you pay it forward?

_____
_____
_____
_____
_____
_____

4. What have you done for your community? What will you do?

_____
_____
_____
_____
_____
_____
_____
_____
_____
_____
_____
_____
_____
_____
_____
_____

Vision Statement: The Man I want to be

Here you will write your personal vision statement. Companies use them to display to their customers & stakeholders, the direction they see the company going in the future. You will use it as a guide to provide direction in your life. Once it is crafted, you will be able to use it to make decisions today that are in alignment with what you want in your future. It should include your most important values, which means this can change from time to time.

Example:

"I dedicate myself to making a commitment to love and cherish my family and friends, to be a leader to my family, in my community and professional roles. I will become a better husband, father, son, friend and man."

Here are a few questions you may want to take into consideration when writing your Personal Vision Statement:

1. What is your definition of success?

_____
_____
_____
_____
_____
_____
_____

2. What did you dream your life would be like?

___

3. What is your life actually like?

___

4. Imagine you pass away at 90 years old, how do you want to be remembered?

_____
_____
_____
_____
_____
_____
_____
_____
_____
_____
_____
_____
_____

_____

5. What are your most important values?

_____
_____
_____
_____
_____
_____
_____
_____

6. What are 3 things you must do daily in order to feel complete in your work?

_____
_____
_____
_____
_____

7. Considering the attributes used here to define men, have you met any MEN in your lifetime that made a positive impact in your life? How did that affect you? In what ways can you pass it forward?

8. Use the space below to craft your Vision Plan.

Notes

Notes

Notes

Notes

www.ingramcontent.com/pod-product-compliance
Lightning Source LLC
Chambersburg PA
CBHW031202090426
42736CB00009B/755